basics to
BRILLIANCE

photography by William Meppem

basics to brilliance
Copyright © Donna Hay Pty Ltd 2016
Design copyright © Donna Hay Pty Ltd 2016
Photographs copyright © William Meppem 2016
Author: Donna Hay
Art direction and design: Chi Lam
Copy editor: Abby Pfahl
Recipes: Donna Hay, Hayley Dodd, Hannah Meppem
Styling and merchandising: Justine Poole
Recipe testers: Maxwell Adey, Dolores Braga Menéndez, Hayley Dodd, Breesa Swann

Fourth Estate
An imprint of HarperCollins*Publishers*

First published in Australia and New Zealand in 2016,
by HarperCollins*Publishers* Australia Pty Limited
ABN 36 009 913 517   harpercollins.com.au

HarperCollins*Publishers*
Level 13, 201 Elizabeth Street, Sydney NSW 2000
Unit D1, 63 Apollo Drive, Rosedale, Auckland 0632, New Zealand
A 53, Sector 57, Noida, UP, India
1 London Bridge Street, London SE1 9GF, United Kingdom
2 Bloor Street East, 20th floor, Toronto, Ontario M4W 1A8, Canada
195 Broadway, New York NY 10007, USA

National Library of Australia cataloguing-in-publication data
Hay, Donna. basics to brilliance / Donna Hay. 1st ed.
ISBN: 978 1 4607 5142 8 (hbk.)
Includes index. Cooking. 641.5

on the cover: garlic bulb, photographed by William Meppem

Reproduction by News PreMedia Centre
Printed and bound in China by RR Donnelley on 140gsm Lucky Bird Uncoated Woodfree
7 6 5   17 18 19

donna hay

basics to
BRILLIANCE

FOURTH ESTATE

CONTENTS

*Ingredients marked with an asterisk have a glossary entry

INTRODUCTION

Just like anything you want to be good at, I believe that mastering the basics is how you build confidence in the kitchen. You have to walk before you can run, right? So, in this book, I'm sharing all my basic recipes with you – my tried and true foundations of the best classics, plus the modern essentials I love and cook all the time. Think the perfect steak, golden roasted chicken, crispy pork belly, my nan's sponge cake and, of course, the fudgiest brownies. Each of these is followed by clever variations and simple flavour change-ups, so one recipe becomes many and your repertoire naturally grows. It's my personal guide to take you from basics to brilliance in the kitchen. Happy cooking!

chapter one

SAVOURY

the basic

BUTTERMILK FRIED CHICKEN

BUTTERMILK FRIED CHICKEN

2 tablespoons sweet paprika*

1 tablespoon fennel seeds, crushed

8 x 125g chicken thigh fillets, trimmed

2 cups (500ml) buttermilk*

vegetable oil, for deep-frying

2 cups (300g) plain (all-purpose) flour

1 tablespoon baking powder

2 teaspoons sea salt flakes, plus extra to serve

½ teaspoon cracked black pepper

STEP 1 Place the paprika and fennel seeds in a large bowl and mix to combine. Add the chicken and toss to coat. Add the buttermilk, mix to combine and refrigerate for 30 minutes.

STEP 2 Fill a large saucepan two-thirds full with oil and place over medium heat until the temperature reaches 180°C (350°F) on a deep-frying thermometer.

STEP 3 While the oil is heating, place the flour, baking powder, salt and pepper on a large tray and toss to combine.

STEP 4 Remove the chicken from the buttermilk mixture, allowing any excess liquid to drip off. Place on the tray with the flour mixture and toss to coat evenly.

STEP 5 Deep-fry the chicken, in batches, for 5–6 minutes or until crisp, golden and cooked through. Drain on paper towel and keep warm. Sprinkle with extra salt to serve. **SERVES 4–6**

TIPS
You can also combine the flour mixture in a large zip-lock plastic bag. Seal and shake to coat the chicken.
To keep the chicken warm before serving, place it on a baking tray in an oven preheated to 140°C (275°F).

crispy chicken burgers

southern-style crispy chicken salad with buttermilk dressing

buttermilk fried chicken and slaw sliders

crispy chicken burgers

½ cup (150g) aioli
1 x quantity buttermilk fried chicken
   (see *basic recipe*), sliced
16 baby cos (romaine) or butter lettuce leaves
2 green tomatoes, sliced
4 dill pickles, sliced
Tabasco Green Pepper Sauce*, to serve
8 burger buns, halved and toasted

Divide the aioli, chicken, lettuce, tomato, pickle
and Tabasco between the bun bases. Sandwich
with the tops of the buns to serve. **MAKES 8**

southern-style crispy chicken salad
with buttermilk dressing

2 baby cos (romaine) lettuces, leaves separated
2 baby fennel bulbs, thinly sliced and fronds reserved
2 Lebanese cucumbers, cut into matchsticks
1 Granny Smith (green) apple, thinly sliced
200g blue cheese, sliced
1 x quantity buttermilk fried chicken
   (see *basic recipe*), sliced
½ x quantity buttermilk dressing (see *basic recipe*, page 211)

Arrange the lettuce, fennel, fennel fronds,
cucumber, apple, cheese and chicken in a large
bowl. Drizzle with the dressing to serve. **SERVES 4**

buttermilk fried chicken and slaw sliders

½ cup (150g) mayonnaise
2 tablespoons lime juice
½ teaspoon finely grated lime rind
4 cups (360g) finely shredded white cabbage
2 green onions (scallions), shredded
1 x quantity buttermilk fried chicken
   (see *basic recipe*), sliced
16 small sesame brioche slider buns*, tops sliced
2 long green chillies, shredded
lime wedges, to serve

Place the mayonnaise, lime juice and lime rind
in a large bowl and mix to combine. Add the cabbage
and onion and toss to combine.
   Divide the slaw and chicken between the buns, top
with the chilli and serve with lime wedges. **MAKES 16**

TIP
*Golden and glossy on the outside
with their fluffy, soft and slightly
sweet centres, brioche buns can
now be found at most supermarkets,
bakeries and major greengrocers.*

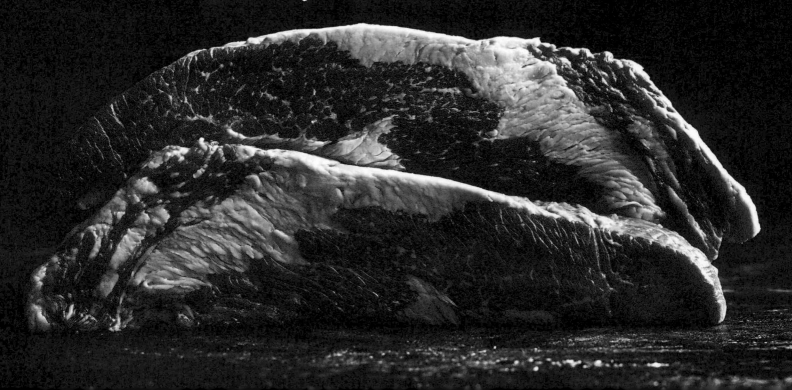

the basic

SLOW-COOKED BEEF BRISKET

SLOW-COOKED BEEF BRISKET

2 tablespoons extra virgin olive oil

1.5kg beef brisket*, trimmed and cut into 4 pieces[+]

1 onion, finely chopped

3 cloves garlic, thinly sliced

1 cup (250ml) red wine

2 cups (500ml) beef stock

2 cups (500ml) water

3 cups (750ml) tomato puree (passata)

6 bay leaves

sea salt and cracked black pepper

STEP 1 Preheat oven to 180°C (350°F).

STEP 2 Heat half the oil in a large ovenproof heavy-based saucepan over medium heat. Add the beef and cook for 4–5 minutes each side or until browned. Remove from the pan and set aside.

STEP 3 Add the remaining oil, the onion and garlic to the pan and cook, stirring, for 4–5 minutes or until softened.

STEP 4 Add the wine and cook for 3–4 minutes or until reduced by half. Add the stock, water, puree, bay leaves, salt and pepper and stir to combine. Return the beef to the pan, with any juices, and bring to a simmer.

STEP 5 Cover with a tight-fitting lid, transfer to the oven and cook, turning the beef halfway through cooking time[++], for 3 hours or until very tender.

STEP 6 Remove the beef from the sauce and place on a tray. Using 2 forks, shred the meat. Return the beef to the sauce and stir to combine. Remove and discard the bay leaves to serve. **SERVES 4–6**

NOTES
+ By cutting the beef into 4 pieces before you begin, you reduce the time it takes to cook.
*++ **For beautifully tender beef that's evenly cooked, ensure you turn it over halfway through the cooking time.***

TIP
This slow-cooked brisket can be made 2–3 days in advance. It freezes well, too – simply thaw and reheat to serve.

brisket pot pies

pappardelle with slow-cooked brisket

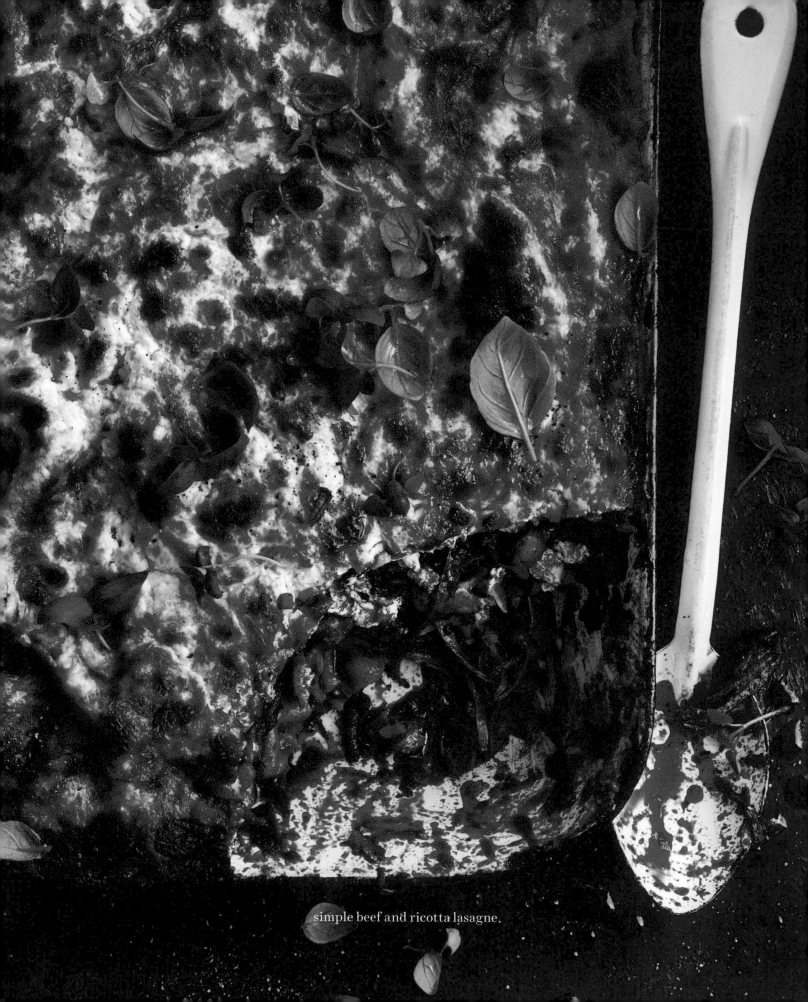

simple beef and ricotta lasagne.

brisket pot pies

1 x quantity slow-cooked beef brisket (see *basic recipe*),
   cooled slightly
3 sheets store-bought puff pastry*
1 egg, lightly beaten

Preheat oven to 200°C (400°F). Divide the beef between
6 x 1-cup-capacity (250ml) ovenproof ramekins. Cut
6 rounds from the pastry to fit the tops of the ramekins.
Cut a small cross incision in the centre of each round.
Brush the edges of the ramekins with egg and top with
the pastry, pressing the edges to seal. Brush the pies
with egg and place on an oven tray. Bake for 30 minutes
or until the pastry is puffed and golden. **MAKES 6**

pappardelle with slow-cooked brisket

500g pappardelle⁺
1 x quantity slow-cooked beef brisket (see *basic recipe*),
   heated through
⅔ cup (50g) finely grated pecorino*
cracked black pepper
baby (micro) parsley, to serve

Cook the pasta in a large saucepan of salted boiling water
for 6–8 minutes or until al dente. Drain well and return to
the pan. Add the beef and toss to combine. Divide between
serving bowls and top with the pecorino. Sprinkle with
pepper and parsley to serve. **SERVES 4–6**

NOTE
*+ Pappardelle is a long, flat, ribbon-shaped
pasta. It goes well with rich, robust sauces like
ragu. Find it dried (or fresh) in supermarkets
and delicatessens, or use your choice of pasta.*

simple beef and ricotta lasagne

3½ cups (350g) grated mozzarella
1¼ cups (100g) finely grated parmesan
4 cups (960g) fresh ricotta
¾ cup (180ml) milk
450g fresh lasagne sheets
1 x quantity slow-cooked beef brisket (see *basic recipe*),
   heated through
2 tablespoons extra virgin olive oil
baby basil leaves, to serve

Preheat oven to 180°C (350°F). Place the mozzarella,
1 cup (80g) of the parmesan, the ricotta and milk in
a large bowl and mix to combine. Set aside.

Line the base of a lightly greased 20cm x 30cm
ovenproof dish with a layer of lasagne sheets, trimming
to fit. Top with one-third of the beef and a second layer
of lasagne sheets. Top with one-third of the cheese
mixture. Repeat the layering twice more using the
remaining lasagne sheets, beef and cheese mixture.

Sprinkle the top layer of cheese mixture with the
remaining parmesan and drizzle with the oil. Place
the dish on an oven tray and bake for 35–40 minutes
or until golden brown and cooked through. Top with
basil leaves to serve. **SERVES 8**

the basic

PERFECT PRAWN DUMPLINGS

steamed prawn dumplings

PERFECT PRAWN DUMPLINGS

12 green (uncooked) prawns (shrimp) (600g), peeled,
deveined and finely chopped[+]

2 tablespoons finely chopped water chestnuts*

2 green onions (scallions), white part only, finely chopped

1 teaspoon finely grated ginger

1 tablespoon finely chopped coriander (cilantro)

1 tablespoon oyster sauce*

1 tablespoon vegetable oil

1 teaspoon table salt

20 gow gee wrappers*

STEP 1 Place the prawn, water chestnut, onion, ginger, coriander, oyster sauce, oil and salt in a medium bowl and mix to combine.

STEP 2 Place 5 of the gow gee wrappers on a clean surface and brush the edges with water[++].

STEP 3 Place 1 heaped teaspoon of the prawn mixture in the centre of each wrapper. Fold the edges over, pinching gently to create pleats, and press together to seal.

STEP 4 Repeat with the remaining gow gee wrappers and prawn mixture[+++]. **MAKES 20**

NOTES

[+] After peeling and deveining the prawns, you should have about 200g prawn meat.

*[++] **Assembling the dumplings in batches helps to prevent the wrappers from drying out in the process. Cover the wrappers you're not using with a clean damp tea towel to keep them workable and soft.***

[+++] See the recipes that follow for how to cook these dumplings.

TIP

Prepared dumplings are great to have on-hand in the freezer. Place them between sheets of non-stick baking paper in an airtight container and freeze for up to 3 months. Cook from frozen as per the recipes that follow.

crispy golden prawn dumplings

ginger, chilli and prawn dumpling soup

prawn pot stickers

steamed prawn dumplings

1 x quantity perfect prawn dumplings (see *basic recipe*)
soy sauce, to serve

Line the base of a large bamboo steamer with a parchment steamer liner[+]. Add half the dumplings to the steamer, ensuring they don't touch. Cover with a tight-fitting lid and place over a large saucepan of simmering water. Steam, misting with water occasionally[++], for 16–18 minutes or until cooked through. Remove from the steamer and keep warm. Repeat with the remaining dumplings. Serve with soy sauce. **MAKES 20**

NOTES

+ Buy bamboo-steamer liners at Asian grocers and some supermarkets. You can also use a round of non-stick baking paper, perforated with holes.
++ Keep dumplings moist and soft as they steam by occasionally misting them with a spray of water.

crispy golden prawn dumplings

vegetable oil, for deep-frying
1 x quantity perfect prawn dumplings (see *basic recipe*)
thinly sliced small red chilli, to serve
chilli oil, to serve

Fill a large saucepan half-full with oil and place over medium heat until the temperature reaches 180°C (350°F) on a deep-frying thermometer. Cook the dumplings, in 4 batches, for 5 minutes or until golden brown and cooked through[+]. Drain on paper towel. Serve with sliced chilli and chilli oil. **MAKES 20**

NOTE

+ Gently stir the dumplings for the first 30 seconds of cooking time to ensure they don't stick together.

ginger, chilli and prawn dumpling soup

2 litres chicken stock
2 teaspoons soy sauce, plus extra to serve
2 tablespoons Chinese cooking wine (Shaoxing)*
2 tablespoons finely shredded ginger
1 x quantity perfect prawn dumplings (see *basic recipe*)
1 long red chilli, seeded and finely shredded
2 green onions (scallions), finely shredded
chilli sauce, to serve

Place the stock, soy sauce, cooking wine and ginger in a large saucepan and bring to the boil. Add half the dumplings and cook for 5 minutes or until cooked through. Using a slotted spoon, remove the dumplings and set aside. Repeat with the remaining dumplings. Divide the dumplings and broth between serving bowls and top with the chilli and onion. Serve with chilli sauce and extra soy sauce. **SERVES 4**

prawn pot stickers

2 tablespoons vegetable oil
1 cup (250ml) chicken stock
1 x quantity perfect prawn dumplings (see *basic recipe*)
Chinese black vinegar, to serve
baby (micro) watercress, to serve

Place half the oil and half the stock in a large non-stick frying pan over medium heat. Bring to the boil and add half the dumplings. Cover with a tight-fitting lid and cook for 5 minutes. Uncover and cook for a further 2–3 minutes or until the stock has evaporated and the dumplings are golden on one side. Remove from the pan and keep warm. Repeat with the remaning oil, stock and dumplings. Serve pot stickers with black vinegar and micro watercress. **MAKES 20**

the basic

QUICK BUTTERFLIED ROAST CHICKEN

QUICK BUTTERFLIED ROAST CHICKEN

1 x 1.6kg whole chicken

4 bulbs garlic, halved horizontally

3 lemons, sliced into 2cm rounds

2 tablespoons extra virgin olive oil

sea salt and cracked black pepper

STEP 1 Preheat oven to 220°C (425°F).

STEP 2 Place the chicken, breast-side down, on a board so the back is facing up and the drumsticks are pointing towards you.

STEP 3 Using sharp kitchen scissors or chicken shears, cut closely along each side of the backbone. Remove and discard the backbone.

STEP 4 Turn the chicken, breast-side up, and press down firmly on the breastbone to flatten the chicken.

STEP 5 Arrange the garlic and lemon on an oven tray lined with non-stick baking paper.

STEP 6 Top with the chicken, breast-side up, tucking in the wing tips.

STEP 7 Brush the chicken with the oil and sprinkle with salt and pepper. Roast for 35–40 minutes or until golden brown and cooked through. **SERVES 4–6**

TIPS
Butterflying a chicken allows it to roast more quickly and evenly.
Placing the chicken on a 'bed' of lemon and garlic infuses it with amazing flavour as it roasts.

roast chicken with crispy sage and bacon lattice

miso-glazed roast chicken

roast chicken with crispy sage and bacon lattice

1 x quantity uncooked quick butterflied roast chicken
   (see *basic recipe*)[+]
2 tablespoons Dijon mustard
12 slices streaky bacon*
10–12 sprigs sage

Preheat oven to 220°C (425°F). Rub the chicken with the mustard and sprinkle with salt and pepper. Drape the bacon over the chicken breast and legs and tuck in the sage sprigs. Drizzle with the oil and roast for 35–40 minutes or until the chicken is golden brown and cooked through and the bacon and sage are crispy. **SERVES 4–6**

NOTE
+ This recipe begins with uncooked butterflied chicken – simply prepare the basic recipe until the end of step 6, keeping the oil on-hand for drizzling and the salt and pepper for sprinkling.

miso-glazed roast chicken

¼ cup (80g) white miso paste*
¼ cup (60ml) mirin (Japanese rice wine)*
1 teaspoon sesame oil
1 x quantity uncooked quick butterflied roast chicken
   (see *basic recipe*)[+]
2 tablespoons peanut oil
1 tablespoon sesame seeds, toasted
2 green onions (scallions), thinly sliced

Preheat oven to 220°C (425°F). Place the miso, mirin and sesame oil in a small bowl and mix until smooth. Brush the glaze evenly over the chicken and drizzle with the peanut oil. Roast, basting with the pan juices occasionally, for 35–40 minutes or until golden and cooked through[++]. Sprinkle with the sesame seeds and onion to serve.
SERVES 4–6

NOTES
+ This recipe begins with uncooked butterflied chicken – simply prepare the basic recipe until the end of step 6.
++ **Cover loosely with foil if turning too dark.**

smoky spice roasted chicken

1 x quantity uncooked quick butterflied roast chicken
   (see *basic recipe*)[+]
smoky spice rub
1 teaspoon fennel seeds
½ teaspoon dried chilli flakes
1 tablespoon smoked paprika*
1 teaspoon ground cumin
1 teaspoon dried thyme leaves
1 teaspoon sea salt flakes
½ teaspoon cracked black pepper

Preheat oven to 220°C (425°F). To make the smoky spice rub, place the fennel seeds and chilli flakes in a mortar and lightly crush with a pestle. Add the paprika, cumin, thyme, salt and pepper and mix to combine.
   Rub the chicken with the spice mixture to coat. Drizzle with the oil and roast, basting with the pan juices occasionally, for 35–40 minutes or until golden brown and cooked through. **SERVES 4–6**

NOTE
+ This recipe begins with uncooked butterflied chicken – prepare the basic recipe until the end of step 6, keeping the oil on-hand for drizzling.

smoky spice roasted chicken

LIGHT AND CRISPY TEMPURA BATTER

mixed tempura vegetables

LIGHT AND CRISPY TEMPURA BATTER

½ cup (75g) cornflour (cornstarch)

½ cup (75g) plain (all-purpose) flour

¼ teaspoon bicarbonate of (baking) soda

1 egg yolk

1 cup (250ml) very cold soda water

STEP 1 Place the cornflour, flour and bicarbonate of soda in a large bowl and mix to combine.

STEP 2 Place the egg yolk and soda water in a small bowl and mix to combine.

STEP 3 Add the egg mixture to the flour mixture and, using 4 chopsticks held together, lightly beat the mixture until just combined but still lumpy. Place the bowl over ice or iced water to keep the batter chilled[+]. **MAKES 1 QUANTITY**

NOTE
+ Keeping the batter icy cold is the best way to ensure it stays light and fluffy. This makes for more delicate, fine and crispy tempura when fried (see the recipes that follow).

crunchy tempura prawns

the perfect tempura fish

mixed tempura vegetables

vegetable oil, for deep-frying
½ cup (75g) plain (all-purpose) flour
1 teaspoon table salt
1 bunch broccolini (tenderstem)* (175g), trimmed
1 sweet potato (kumara) (600g), peeled and sliced
    into 5mm rounds
4 zucchini (courgette) flowers (40g), halved lengthways
100g green beans, trimmed
1 bunch asparagus (175g), trimmed
1 x quantity light and crispy tempura batter (see *basic recipe*)
dipping sauce
¼ cup (60ml) soy sauce
2 tablespoons mirin (Japanese rice wine)*
1 tablespoon lemon juice
1 teaspoon finely shredded ginger

To make the dipping sauce, place the soy sauce,
mirin, lemon juice and ginger in a small bowl and
mix to combine. Set aside.

Fill a large saucepan half-full with oil and place
over medium heat until the temperature reaches
190°C (375°F) on a deep-frying thermometer.

Place the flour and salt in a medium bowl and mix
to combine. Dust the vegetables in the flour mixture.
Working in batches, dip the vegetables in the batter
and deep-fry for 2–3 minutes or until golden brown
and cooked through. Drain on paper towel. Place on
a serving plate and serve with the dipping sauce.
SERVES 4 AS A STARTER OR SIDE

crunchy tempura prawns

vegetable oil, for deep-frying
½ cup (75g) plain (all-purpose) flour
1 teaspoon table salt
600g green (uncooked) prawns (shrimp), peeled and
    deveined with tails intact
1 x quantity light and crispy tempura batter (see *basic recipe*)
dipping sauce
¼ cup (60ml) soy sauce
2 tablespoons mirin (Japanese rice wine)*
2 tablespoons lemon juice
1 green onion (scallion), thinly sliced
1 small red chilli, thinly sliced

To make the dipping sauce, place the soy sauce, mirin,
lemon juice, onion and chilli in a small bowl and mix to
combine. Set aside. Fill a large saucepan half-full with
oil and place over medium heat until the temperature
reaches 190°C (375°F) on a deep-frying thermometer.

Place the flour and salt in a medium bowl and mix to
combine. Dust the prawns in the flour mixture. Working
in batches, dip the prawns in the batter and deep-fry for
1–2 minutes or until golden brown and cooked through.
Drain on paper towel. Divide between serving bowls and
serve with the dipping sauce. **SERVES 4 AS A STARTER OR SIDE**

the perfect tempura fish

vegetable oil, for deep-frying
½ cup (75g) plain (all-purpose) flour
1 teaspoon table salt
600g sand whiting fillets or any firm white fish fillets,
    pin-boned
1 x quantity light and crispy tempura batter (see *basic recipe*)
baby (micro) shiso and watercress, to serve
ponzu sauce*, wasabi, pickled ginger* and sea salt, to serve

Fill a large saucepan half-full with oil and place over
medium heat until the temperature reaches 190°C (375°F)
on a deep-frying thermometer.

Place the flour and salt in a medium bowl and mix to
combine. Dust the fish in the flour mixture. Working
in batches, dip the fish in the batter and deep-fry for
1–2 minutes or until golden brown and cooked through.
Drain on paper towel. Divide between serving plates and
sprinkle with shiso and watercress. Serve with ponzu
sauce, wasabi, pickled ginger and salt. **SERVES 4**

the basic

PERFECTLY COOKED STEAKS

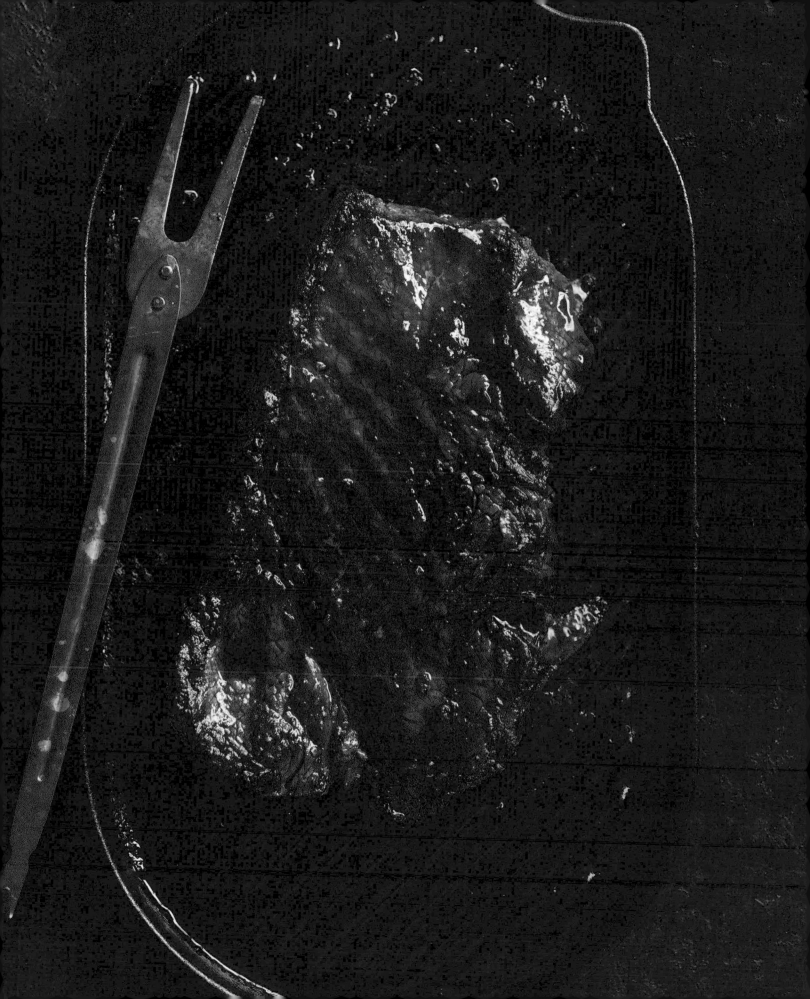

PERFECTLY COOKED STEAKS

2 x 4cm -thick rump steaks or boneless sirloin steaks (700g)

1 tablespoon extra virgin olive oil

2 cups (600g) rock salt

cracked black pepper

STEP 1 Rub the steaks with the oil.

STEP 2 Spread half the rock salt over a tray, top with the steaks and cover with the remaining salt. Set aside for 20 minutes.

STEP 3 Wipe all the salt from the steaks, using paper towel, and sprinkle with pepper.

STEP 4 Preheat a char-grill pan or barbecue over high heat.

STEP 5 Cook the steaks, turning every 1 minute, for 2–3 minutes each side or until cooked to your liking.

STEP 6 Cover gently with aluminium foil and allow to rest for 5 minutes before serving. **SERVES 4**

TIPS

Salting the steaks helps to tenderise the beef and adds to its flavour.
Turning the steaks ensures they cook evenly and caramelise on the outside.
Slice the cooked steaks thickly and serve with hand-cut chips and mustard.

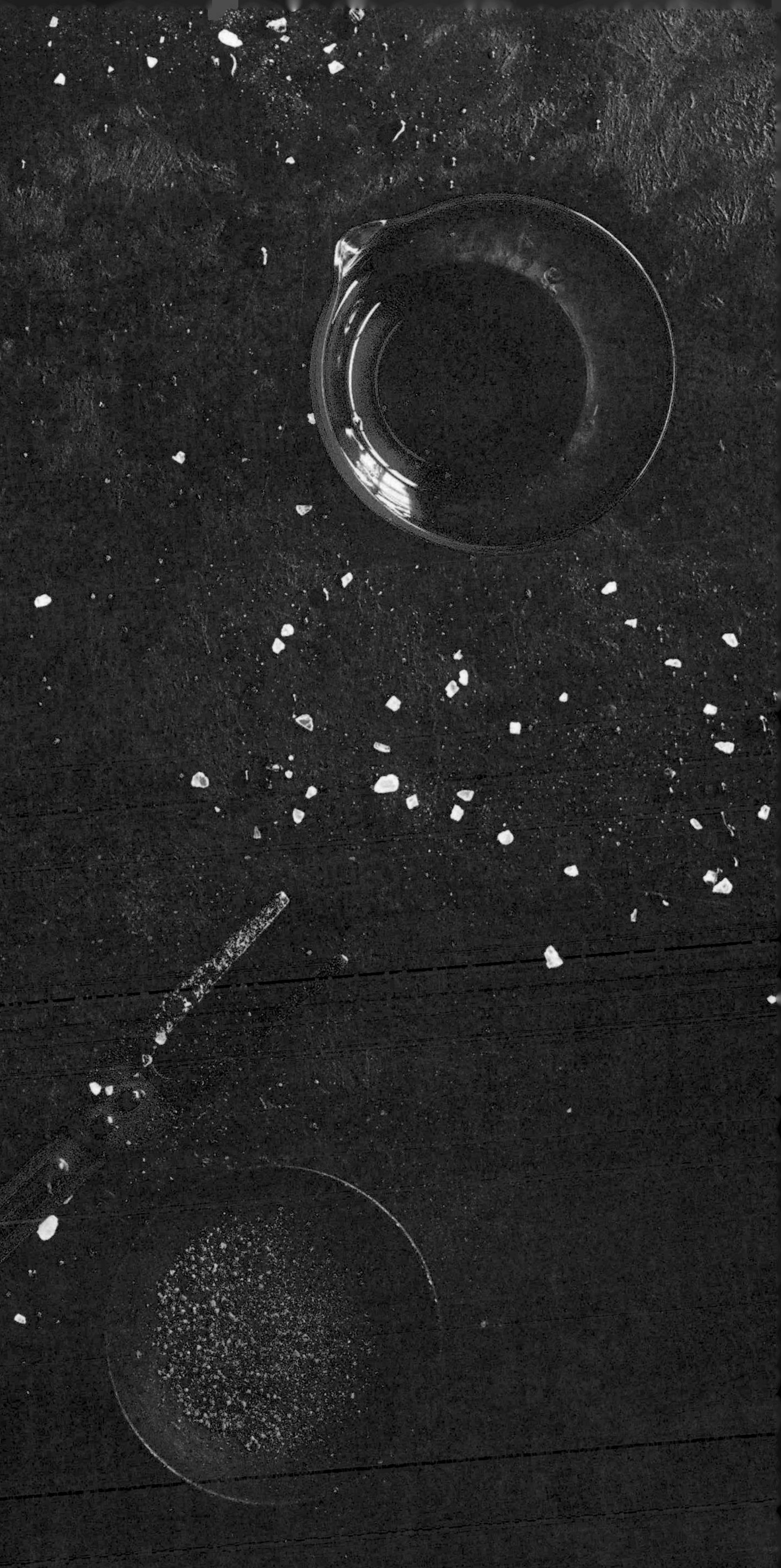

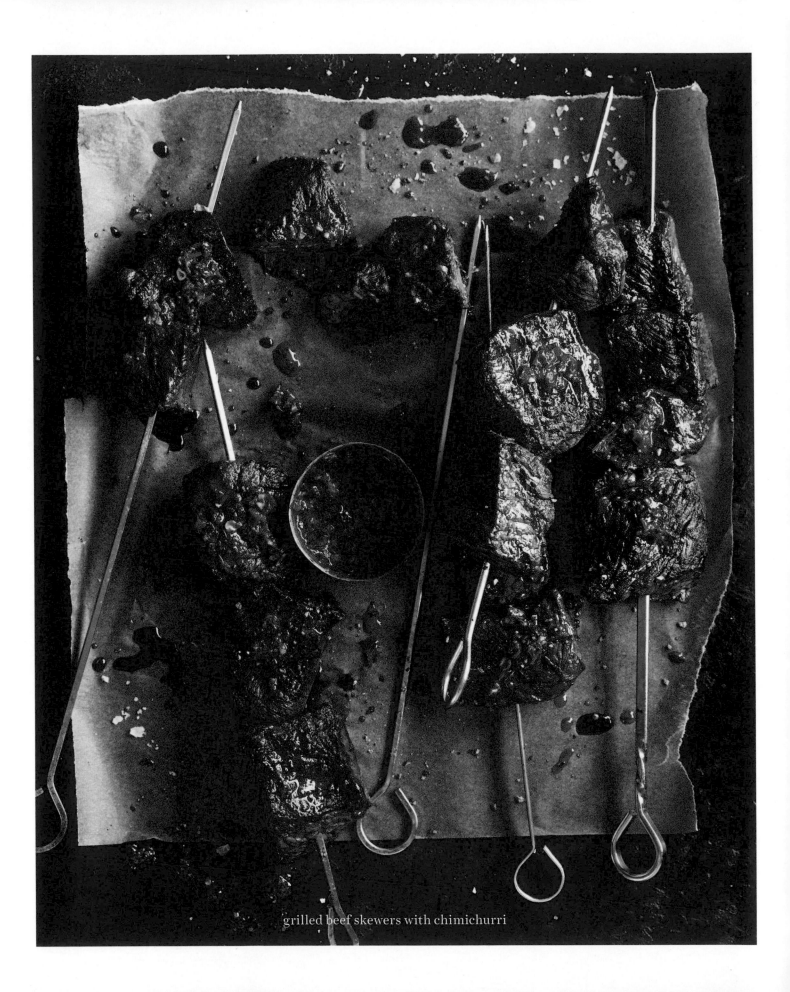

grilled beef skewers with chimichurri

the ultimate steak sandwich

grilled beef skewers with chimichurri

1 x quantity uncooked perfectly cooked steaks
   (see *basic recipe*)+
chimichurri
½ cup coriander (cilantro) leaves
½ cup flat-leaf parsley leaves
¼ cup oregano leaves
1 long green chilli, chopped
1 clove garlic
¼ cup (60ml) extra virgin olive oil
2 tablespoons red wine vinegar
sea salt and cracked black pepper

To make the chimichurri, place the coriander, parsley,
oregano, chilli, garlic, oil, vinegar, salt and pepper in a
small food processor and process until finely chopped
and smooth. Set aside.

Preheat a char-grill pan or barbecue over high heat.
Cut the steaks into 5cm pieces. Thread 2–3 pieces of beef
onto each metal skewer. Cook, turning every 1–2 minutes,
for 6–8 minutes or until cooked to your liking. Serve with
the chimichurri. **SERVES 4**

NOTE
+ *This recipe begins with uncooked steak – simply
prepare the basic recipe until the end of step 3.*

the ultimate steak sandwich

¼ cup (60ml) apple cider vinegar
2 tablespoons caster (superfine) sugar
½ teaspoon sea salt flakes
1 red onion, thinly sliced
8 slices sourdough bread, lightly toasted
⅓ cup (90g) tomato relish
8 slices vintage cheddar
1 x quantity perfectly cooked steaks (see *basic recipe*),
   thinly sliced
8 cos (romaine) or butter lettuce leaves

Place the vinegar, sugar and salt in a medium bowl and
stir until the sugar has dissolved. Add the onion and toss
to combine. Set aside for 15 minutes to pickle.

Spread the sourdough slices with the relish. Top 4 of the
slices with the cheddar, steak, onion and lettuce. Sandwich
with the remaining sourdough to serve. **MAKES 4**

spicy korean steak tacos with kimchi

1 x quantity uncooked perfectly cooked steaks
   (see *basic recipe*)+
16 small flour tortillas, lightly toasted
½ cup (150g) Japanese mayonnaise*
2 cups (160g) finely shredded daikon*
1 cup (200g) store-bought kimchi*
½ cup coriander (cilantro) leaves
spicy ginger sauce
2 tablespoons oyster sauce*
1 tablespoon Chinese cooking wine (Shaoxing)*
1 tablespoon finely grated ginger
1 teaspoon dried chilli flakes
1 tablespoon finely grated palm sugar* or brown sugar

To make the spicy ginger sauce, place the oyster sauce,
cooking wine, ginger, chilli flakes and sugar in a small
bowl and mix until the sugar has dissolved.

Preheat a char-grill pan or barbecue over high heat.
Cook the steaks, turning every 1 minute, for 2–3 minutes
each side or until cooked to your liking. In the last
30 seconds of cooking time, brush the steaks with the
spicy ginger sauce and turn to caramelise both sides.
Cover gently with aluminium foil and allow to rest for
5 minutes. Thinly slice the steaks.

Spread the tortillas with the mayonnaise. Top with
the daikon, steak, kimchi and coriander to serve. **MAKES 16**

NOTE
+ *This recipe begins with uncooked steak – simply
prepare the basic recipe until the end of step 3.*
TIP
*Turning the steaks ensures they cook evenly
and caramelise on the outside.*

spicy korean steak tacos with kimchi

the basic

THAI GREEN CURRY PASTE

THAI GREEN CURRY PASTE

1 teaspoon cumin seeds

1 tablespoon coriander seeds

3 long green chillies, roughly chopped

2 cloves garlic

30g galangal* or ginger, peeled and chopped

6 kaffir lime leaves*, stems removed and shredded

2 stalks lemongrass*, white part only,
thinly sliced

1 cup chopped coriander (cilantro) leaves,
stems and roots+

1 tablespoon peanut or vegetable oil

½ teaspoon shrimp paste*

1 tablespoon grated palm sugar* or brown sugar

3 green onions (scallions), roughly chopped

STEP 1 Heat a small non-stick frying pan over medium heat. Add the cumin and coriander seeds and toast, shaking the pan frequently, for 2–3 minutes or until fragrant and light golden.

STEP 2 Place in a small food processor and process until ground.

STEP 3 Add the chilli, garlic, galangal, lime leaf, lemongrass, chopped coriander, the oil, shrimp paste, sugar and onion. Process into a paste, scraping down the sides of the bowl. **MAKES 1 QUANTITY**

NOTE
+ You'll need approximately 3 roots (50g) of coriander to get 1 cup of chopped coriander.
TIP
Keep this curry paste in a jar in the refrigerator for up to 1 week.

thai-style pork and basil curry

fragrant green chicken curry

thai-style pork and basil curry

1 x quantity Thai green curry paste (see *basic recipe*)
1 x 400ml can coconut milk*
1 cup (250ml) chicken stock
800g boneless pork neck, trimmed and sliced into 1cm strips
2 tablespoons fish sauce*
1 cup purple basil leaves
1 cup Thai basil leaves
1 green onion (scallion), finely shredded
garlic chives, to serve
store-bought crispy fried shallots (eschalots), to serve

Place a large saucepan over medium heat. Add the curry paste and cook, stirring frequently, for 2–3 minutes or until fragrant. Add the coconut milk and stock, stir to combine and bring to a simmer. Add the pork, return to a simmer and cook for 5 minutes or until the pork is cooked through. Add the fish sauce and stir to combine.

Divide the curry between serving bowls and top with the basil, onion, chives and crispy shallots. **SERVES 4**

fragrant green chicken curry

1 x quantity Thai green curry paste (see *basic recipe*)
1 x 400ml can coconut milk*
1 cup (250ml) chicken stock
8 x 125g chicken thigh fillets, trimmed and quartered
2 tablespoons fish sauce*
4 kaffir lime leaves*, stems removed and finely shredded
½ cup coriander (cilantro) leaves
½ cup (80g) roasted cashews, roughly chopped
1 long green chilli, thinly sliced
1 x quantity white rice (see *basic recipe*, page 216)
lime wedges, to serve

Place a large saucepan over medium heat. Add the curry paste and cook, stirring frequently, for 2–3 minutes or until fragrant. Add the coconut milk and stock, stir to combine and bring to a simmer. Add the chicken, return to a simmer and cook for 5–8 minutes or until the chicken is cooked through. Add the fish sauce and stir to combine.

Top the curry with the lime leaf, coriander, cashews and chilli. Serve with the rice and lime wedges. **SERVES 4**

spicy green curry prawns with noodles

1 x quantity Thai green curry paste (see *basic recipe*)
1 x 400ml can coconut milk*
1 cup (250ml) chicken stock
24 green (uncooked) king prawns (shrimp) (1.2kg), peeled and deveined with tails intact
2 tablespoons fish sauce*
200g dried rice noodles, cooked according to packet instructions
½ cup baby (micro) purple basil
1 cup baby (micro) coriander (cilantro)
chilli oil, to serve

Place a large saucepan over medium heat. Add the curry paste and cook, stirring frequently, for 2–3 minutes or until fragrant. Add the coconut milk and stock, stir to combine and bring to a simmer. Add the prawns, return to a simmer and cook for 2–3 minutes or until the prawns are cooked through. Add the fish sauce and stir to combine.

Divide the noodles and curry between serving bowls and top with the basil, coriander and chilli oil to serve. **SERVES 4**

TIP
Serve these fragrant Thai-style curries with rice noodles or steamed jasmine rice.

spicy green curry prawns with noodles

CRISPY ROASTED PORK BELLY

CRISPY ROASTED PORK BELLY

1kg boneless pork belly

1 tablespoon sea salt flakes

1 tablespoon extra virgin olive oil

1 onion, sliced into 1cm rounds

1 lemon, sliced into 1cm rounds

STEP 1 Preheat oven to 180°C (350°F).

STEP 2 Using a small sharp knife, score the pork skin at 1cm intervals.

STEP 3 Pat the skin dry with paper towel[+]. Rub the salt and oil into the skin and incisions.

STEP 4 Place the pork, skin-side down, on an oven tray and roast for 1 hour 30 minutes.

STEP 5 Remove the pork from the oven and increase the oven temperature to 220°C (425°F).

STEP 6 Working quickly, arrange the onion and lemon on the oven tray next to the pork. Turn the pork over onto the onion and lemon. Roast for a further 20–30 minutes or until the skin is golden and crispy and the meat is tender. **SERVES 4**

NOTE

+ For the crunchiest pork crackling, be sure to thoroughly dry the skin. If you have the time, you can refrigerate the pork, uncovered, for 2 hours or overnight. This will let the skin dry out even further, before you oil and salt the rind.

pork belly banh mi

asian-style pork belly pancakes

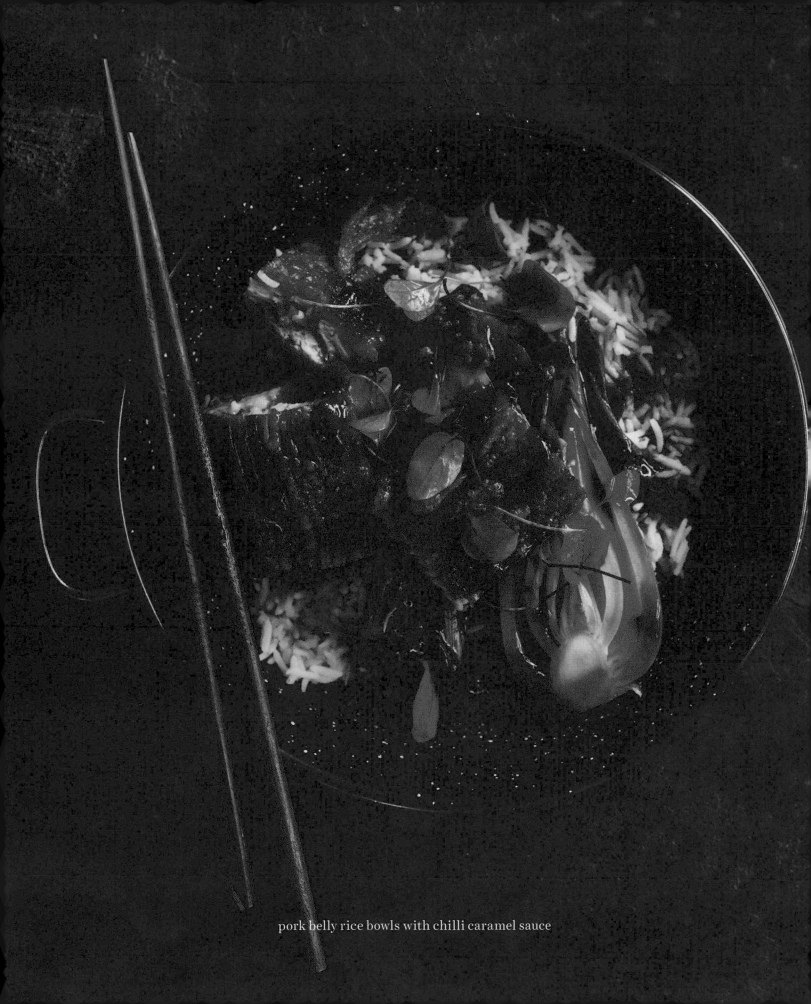

pork belly rice bowls with chilli caramel sauce

pork belly banh mi

¼ cup (60ml) rice wine vinegar
2 tablespoons caster (superfine) sugar
1 teaspoon sea salt flakes
2 Lebanese cucumbers, thinly sliced
6 long white crusty bread rolls, tops sliced
1 x quantity crispy roasted pork belly (see *basic recipe*), sliced
½ cup mint leaves
2 long green chillies, thinly sliced
chilli sauce and mayonnaise, to serve

Place the vinegar, sugar and salt in a medium bowl and whisk until the sugar has dissolved. Add the cucumber, toss to combine and set aside for 10 minutes to pickle.

Drain the cucumber and divide between the rolls with the pork, mint and chilli. Top with chilli sauce and mayonnaise to serve. **SERVES 6**

asian-style pork belly pancakes

¼ cup (60ml) rice wine vinegar
2 tablespoons caster (superfine) sugar
1 teaspoon sea salt flakes
1½ cups (120g) shredded daikon*
1 cup (70g) shredded Lebanese cucumber
20 store-bought Chinese pancakes*
1 x quantity crispy roasted pork belly (see *basic recipe*), meat shredded and crackling sliced
½ cup (125ml) hoisin sauce*
thinly sliced long green chilli, to serve

Place the vinegar, sugar and salt in a medium bowl and whisk until the sugar has dissolved. Add the daikon and cucumber, toss to combine and set aside to pickle for 10 minutes.

While the vegetables are pickling, warm the pancakes according to packet instructions.

Divide the pork and crackling between the pancakes. Top with the pickled vegetables, hoisin sauce and chilli. Wrap to enclose to serve. **MAKES 20**

TIP
For extra freshness and crunch, you can add finely shredded Chinese cabbage (wombok) to these pancakes to serve.

pork belly rice bowls with chilli caramel sauce

1½ cups (300g) jasmine rice
2¼ cups (560ml) water
sea salt
1 x quantity crispy roasted pork belly (see *basic recipe*), heated through and cut into 4cm squares
6 baby bok choy* (900g), halved and steamed
red-veined sorrel leaves, to serve
chilli caramel sauce
1 cup (220g) white (granulated) sugar
¼ cup (60ml) fish sauce*
¼ cup (60ml) water
1 tablespoon finely grated ginger
2 cloves garlic, crushed
1 long red chilli, shredded
1 tablespoon rice wine vinegar

Place the rice, water and salt in a medium saucepan over high heat and bring to the boil. Cover with a tight-fitting lid, reduce the heat to low and simmer for 12 minutes. Remove from the heat and allow to steam for 8 minutes.

While the rice is cooking, make the chilli caramel sauce. Place the sugar in a large heavy-based saucepan over medium heat and cook, swirling the pan occasionally (do not stir), for 8–10 minutes or until golden caramel in colour and all the sugar has dissolved. Remove from the heat, carefully add the fish sauce and water and stir to combine. Return to medium heat, add the ginger, garlic and chilli and bring to a simmer. Cook for 5–8 minutes or until thickened and syrupy. Remove from the heat, add the vinegar and stir to combine.

Divide the rice, pork, bok choy and the sauce between serving bowls and top with sorrel leaves to serve. **SERVES 4**

the basic
___

ASIAN-STYLE POACHED CHICKEN

ASIAN-STYLE POACHED CHICKEN

5 green onions (scallions), cut into 3 pieces

1 brown onion, quartered

2 long red chillies, halved

100g ginger, peeled and sliced

6 cloves garlic, bruised

¼ cup (60ml) light soy sauce

1 cup (250ml) Chinese cooking wine (Shaoxing)*

¼ cup (55g) caster (superfine) sugar

4 litres water

1 x 1.8kg whole chicken

STEP 1 Place the green onion, brown onion, chilli, ginger, garlic, soy sauce, cooking wine, sugar and water in a large saucepan over high heat. Stir to combine and bring to the boil.

STEP 2 Add the chicken, breast-side down. Reduce the heat to low and cook for 30 minutes.

STEP 3 Remove from the heat, cover with a tight-fitting lid and allow to stand for 1 hour.

STEP 4 Remove the chicken from the stock and allow to cool slightly. Shred the chicken, discarding the skin and bones, and set aside.

STEP 5 Strain the stock into a large heatproof bowl, discarding the solids. Allow to cool. Skim any excess fat from the surface. **MAKES 1 QUANTITY**

TIPS

Use the flavourful shredded chicken in soups, sandwiches and salads.

You can freeze the chicken stock in airtight containers for up to 3 months. Thaw it to use in anything from Asian-flavoured soup bases to fragrant noodle dishes. It's also perfect for poaching chicken breasts in for extra-tasty salads, sandwiches and rolls.

ginger and sesame chicken noodle bowls

feel-good chicken soup

chicken, green papaya and lime salad

ginger and sesame chicken noodle bowls

440g fresh flat rice noodles+
1 x quantity shredded Asian-style poached chicken
   (see *basic recipe*), heated through
2 cups (500ml) Asian-style poached chicken stock
   (see *basic recipe*), heated through
1 tablespoon sesame seeds, toasted
3 green onions (scallions), thinly sliced
1 long red chilli, thinly sliced
1 cup coriander (cilantro) leaves
ginger dressing
1 tablespoon soy sauce
1 tablespoon sesame oil
1 tablespoon finely grated ginger
1 green onion (scallion), chopped

To make the ginger dressing, place the soy sauce,
oil, ginger and chopped onion in a small bowl.
Mix to combine and set aside.

Place the noodles in a medium heatproof bowl
and cover with boiling water. Allow to stand for
2 minutes. Gently separate the noodles, using a
fork, and drain well.

Divide the noodles, chicken and stock between
serving bowls and top with the ginger dressing.
Sprinkle with the sesame seeds, sliced onion,
chilli and coriander to serve. **SERVES 4**

NOTE
+ *Fresh rice noodles are sold in*
packs in the chilled section of your
supermarket or Asian grocer.
You can use dried rice noodles,
if you prefer – simply soften them
according to packet instructions.

feel-good chicken soup

2 litres Asian-style poached chicken stock
   (see *basic recipe*)
1 tablespoon finely shredded ginger
2 tablespoons soy sauce
1 bunch gai lan (Chinese broccoli)* (300g), trimmed
1 x quantity shredded Asian-style poached chicken
   (see *basic recipe*), heated through
3 green onions (scallions), sliced
2 long green chillies, thinly sliced

Place the stock, ginger and soy sauce in a large
saucepan over high heat and bring to the boil. Add
the gai lan and cook for 1 minute or until just tender.

Divide the chicken, onion and chilli between
serving bowls and ladle the broth and gai lan over
to serve. **SERVES 4**

chicken, green papaya and lime salad

¼ cup (60ml) lime juice
2 tablespoons brown sugar
2 tablespoons fish sauce*
1 x quantity shredded Asian-style poached chicken
   (see *basic recipe*), cooled
1 green papaya*, peeled, seeded and finely shredded
1 Lebanese cucumber, peeled and finely shredded
2 radishes, thinly sliced
1 cup Thai basil leaves
½ cup (70g) salted roasted peanuts, chopped
lime wedges, to serve

Place the lime juice, sugar and fish sauce in a large
bowl and mix until the sugar has dissolved. Add the
chicken, papaya, cucumber, radish, basil and peanuts
and toss to combine. Divide between serving bowls
and serve with lime wedges. **SERVES 4**

the basic

CHEAT'S RICOTTA GNOCCHI DOUGH

CHEAT'S RICOTTA GNOCCHI DOUGH

1½ cups (360g) fresh ricotta[+]

1 cup (80g) finely grated parmesan

1 cup (150g) plain (all-purpose) flour

3 eggs

1½ teaspoons sea salt flakes

cracked black pepper

STEP 1 Place the ricotta, parmesan, flour, eggs, salt and pepper in a large bowl. Mix until combined and a sticky dough forms. **MAKES 1 QUANTITY**

—

NOTE

+ *For the best results, buy fresh full-cream ricotta. It's available at delicatessens and the deli counter of supermarkets.*

TIP

This dough should be a little sticky to work with. Keep some extra flour on-hand for dusting when it comes time to shape and slice the gnocchi in the recipes that follow.

simple spinach and ricotta gnocchi

herb, ricotta and cherry tomato gnocchi

simple spinach and ricotta gnocchi

1 teaspoon finely grated lemon rind
¼ cup (60ml) lemon juice
2 tablespoons extra virgin olive oil
sea salt and cracked black pepper
300g baby spinach leaves
1 x quantity cheat's ricotta gnocchi dough (see *basic recipe*)
wild rocket (arugula) leaves and shaved parmesan, to serve

Place the lemon rind, lemon juice, oil, salt and pepper in
a medium bowl. Mix to combine and set aside.
　Place the spinach in a large heatproof bowl, cover with
boiling water and set aside for 1 minute. Drain, place in a
clean tea towel, squeeze to remove the excess liquid and
finely chop. Add the spinach to the gnocchi dough and mix
to combine. Lightly dust a clean surface with flour. Divide
the dough in half and roll each piece into a 3cm-wide log.
Slice into 2cm-thick pieces and set aside on a lightly
floured tray. Cook the gnocchi, in 2 batches, in a large
saucepan of salted boiling water for 2–3 minutes or until
risen to the surface. Remove with a slotted spoon and place
on a serving plate. Top with the lemon oil, rocket and
parmesan to serve. **SERVES 4**

herb, ricotta and cherry tomato gnocchi

¼ cup each finely chopped basil and flat-leaf parsley leaves
1 tablespoon finely chopped thyme leaves
1 tablespoon finely grated lemon rind
1 x quantity cheat's ricotta gnocchi dough (see *basic recipe*)
¼ cup (60ml) extra virgin olive oil
3 cloves garlic, sliced
600g mixed cherry tomatoes
finely grated parmesan and baby (micro) basil, to serve

Add the chopped herbs and lemon rind to the gnocchi
dough and mix to combine. Lightly dust a clean surface
with flour. Divide the dough in half and roll each piece
into a 3cm-wide log. Slice into 2cm-thick pieces and set
aside on a lightly floured tray.
　Heat the oil in a large non-stick frying pan over high
heat. Add the garlic and tomatoes and cook for 5 minutes
or until soft. Cook the gnocchi, in 2 batches, in a large
saucepan of salted boiling water for 2–3 minutes or until
firm and risen to the surface. Remove with a slotted
spoon and toss in the pan with the tomatoes. Serve with
the parmesan and baby basil. **SERVES 4**

roasted garlic and ricotta gnocchi with sage burnt butter

2 bulbs garlic, halved
1 tablespoon extra virgin olive oil
sea salt and cracked black pepper
1 x quantity cheat's ricotta gnocchi dough (see *basic recipe*)
125g unsalted butter
1½ cups sage leaves
finely grated parmesan, to serve
lemon wedges, to serve

Preheat oven to 200°C (400°F). Place the garlic, cut-side
up, on a sheet of aluminium foil. Drizzle with the oil and
sprinkle with salt and pepper. Wrap to enclose and roast
for 40 minutes or until soft. Set aside to cool slightly.
　Squeeze the roasted garlic cloves from their skins.
Place half the cloves in a small bowl and mash well,
using a fork, reserving the remaining cloves.
　Add the mashed garlic to the gnocchi dough and mix
well to combine. Lightly dust a clean surface with flour.
Divide the dough in half and roll each piece into a
3cm-wide log. Slice into 4cm-thick pieces and set aside
on a lightly floured tray.
　Melt the butter in a large non-stick frying pan over
medium heat. Add the sage and cook for 2–3 minutes or
until crisp. Remove the sage from the pan and set aside.
　Cook the gnocchi, in 2 batches, in a large saucepan of
salted boiling water for 2–3 minutes or until firm and
risen to the surface. Remove with a slotted spoon, transfer
to the pan with the butter and cook for 2–3 minutes each
side or until golden brown and crisp. Divide the gnocchi
and burnt butter between serving plates and top with the
sage and reserved garlic cloves. Sprinkle with salt and
parmesan and serve with lemon wedges. **SERVES 4**

roasted garlic and ricotta gnocchi with sage burnt butter

the basic

SMOKY PULLED PORK

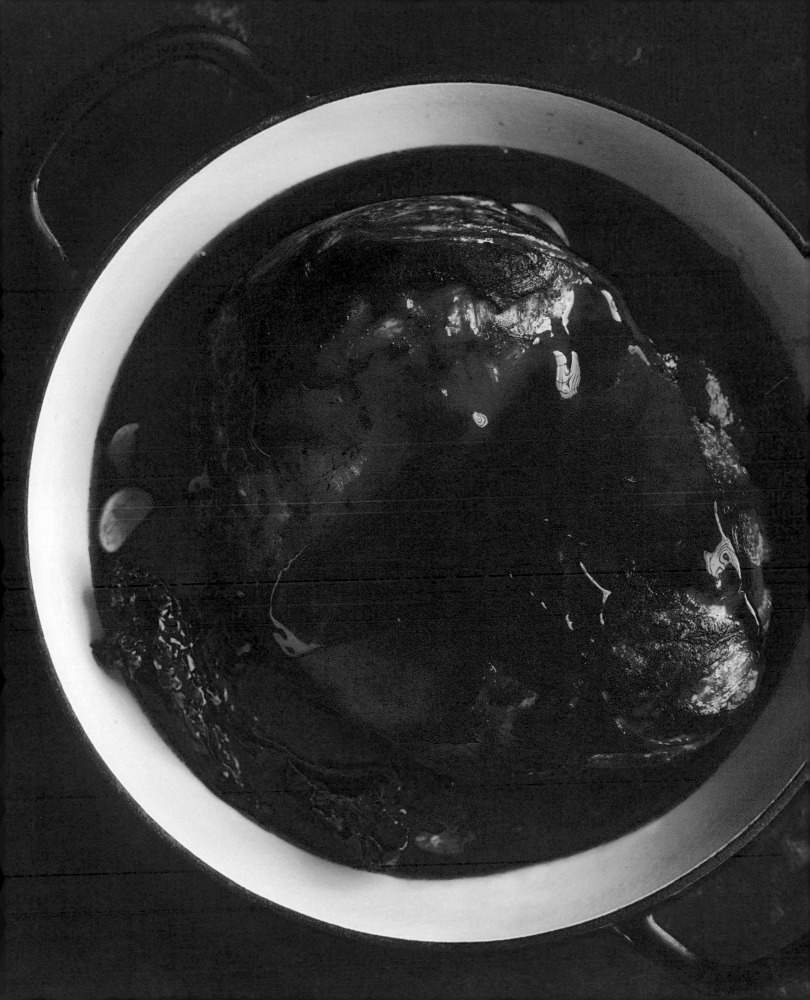

SMOKY PULLED PORK

1 tablespoon extra virgin olive oil

1kg boneless pork shoulder,
rind removed and trimmed

sea salt and cracked black pepper

1 cup (250ml) tomato puree (passata)

1 cup (250ml) beef stock

1 cup (250ml) water

1 cup (250ml) bourbon or dark rum

¼ cup (60ml) malt vinegar

¼ cup (60ml) maple syrup

4 cloves garlic, sliced

2 dried ancho chillies*, roughly chopped

2 teaspoons smoked paprika*

½ teaspoon dried chilli flakes

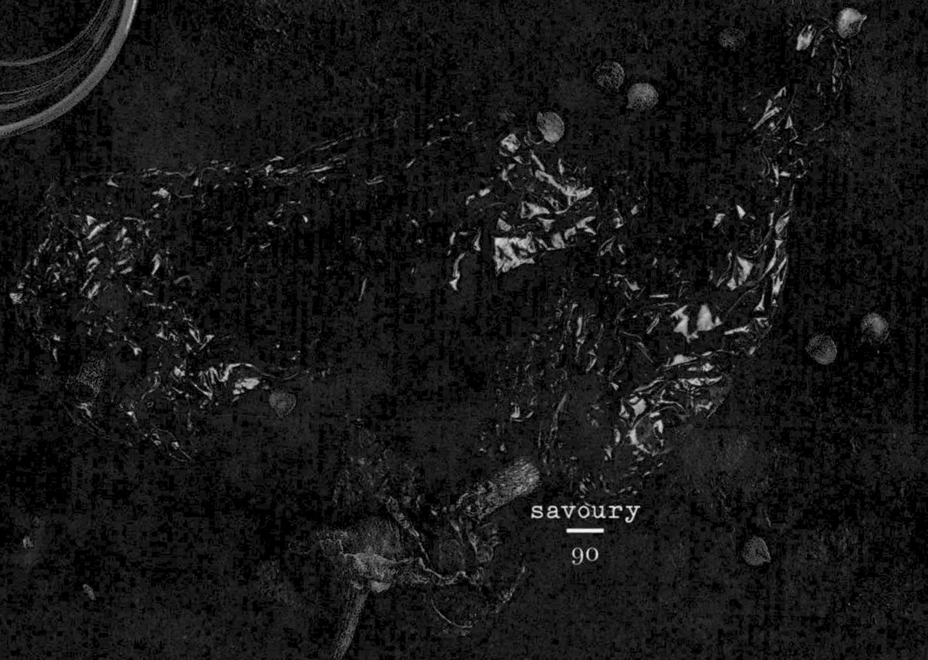

STEP 1 Preheat oven to 180°C (350°F).

STEP 2 Heat the oil in a large ovenproof heavy-based saucepan over high heat. Sprinkle the pork with salt and pepper and cook for 5 minutes each side or until well browned.

STEP 3 Add the puree, stock, water, bourbon, vinegar, maple syrup, garlic, chilli, paprika and chilli flakes. Stir to combine and bring to a simmer.

STEP 4 Cover with a tight-fitting lid and transfer to the oven. Cook for 1 hour 30 minutes.

STEP 5 Turn the pork over, return to the oven and cook, covered, for a further 1 hour 30 minutes or until tender.

STEP 6 Remove the pork from the sauce and place on a tray. Using 2 forks, shred the meat and discard any fat.

STEP 7 Return the pork to the sauce to serve. **SERVES 6**

mexican pulled pork tacos

easy pork empanadas

mexican pulled pork tacos

12 small flour tortillas
1 x quantity smoky pulled pork (see *basic recipe*),
    heated through
3 cups (180g) shredded iceberg lettuce
1 green tomato, sliced
¼ cup (60g) sliced jalapeños*
½ red onion, thinly sliced
1 avocado, thinly sliced
½ cup coriander (cilantro) leaves
lime wedges, to serve

Heat each tortilla in a small non-stick frying pan
over medium heat for 30 seconds each side.
    Divide the pork, lettuce, tomato, jalapeño,
onion, avocado and coriander between the tortillas.
Fold and serve with lime wedges. **MAKES 12**

easy pork empanadas

5 sheets store-bought shortcrust pastry*
1 x quantity smoky pulled pork (see *basic recipe*), cooled
1 egg, lightly beaten
2 teaspoons sesame seeds

Preheat oven to 200°C (400°F). Cut 4 x 12cm rounds
from each pastry sheet. Place 2 tablespoons of the pork
in the centre of each round and brush the edges with the
egg. Fold the pastry over to enclose the pork and press
the edges to seal, folding and pinching to create a ruffle.
    Place the empanadas on lightly greased baking trays
lined with non-stick baking paper and brush with the
egg. Sprinkle with the sesame seeds and bake for
20–25 minutes or until golden. Serve warm. **MAKES 20**

southern-style pulled pork and slaw sliders

4 cups (320g) shredded white cabbage
1 baby fennel bulb, finely shredded and
    fronds reserved
1 carrot, peeled and finely shredded
¼ cup (75g) mayonnaise
1 x quantity smoky pulled pork (see *basic recipe*),
    heated through
20 brioche slider buns*, halved

Place the cabbage, fennel, carrot and mayonnaise
in a large bowl and toss until well combined.
    Divide the pork, slaw and reserved fennel fronds
between the bases of the buns. Sandwich with the
tops of the buns to serve. **MAKES 20**

TIPS
*Golden and glossy on the outside
with their fluffy, soft and slightly
sweet centres, brioche buns can
now be found at most supermarkets,
bakeries and major greengrocers.*
**You can make the smoky pulled
pork in advance – it will keep in
the freezer for up to 3 months.**

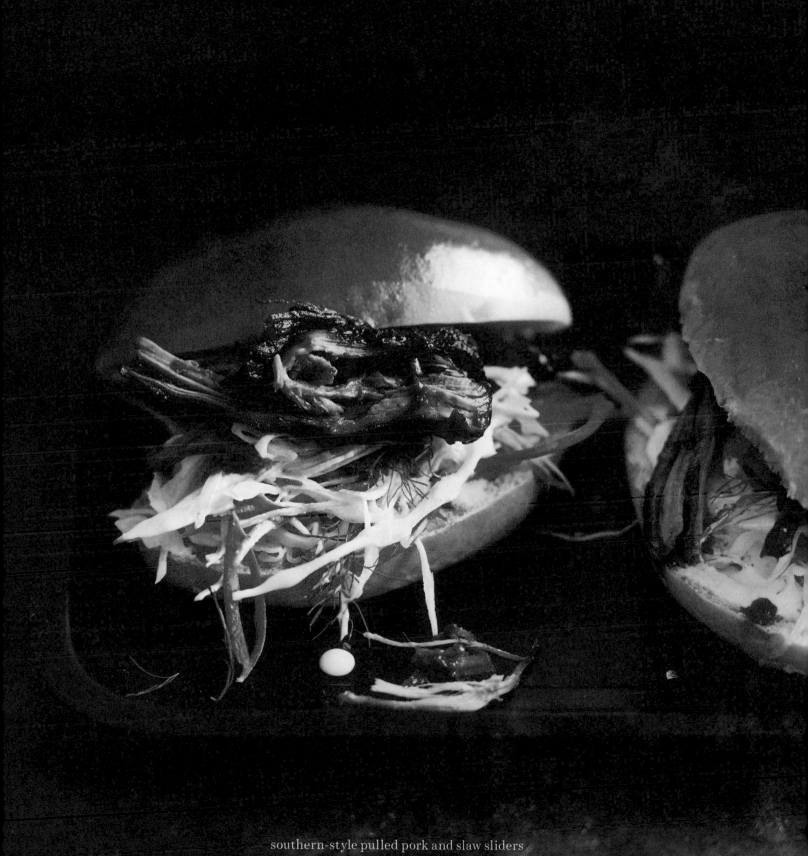

southern-style pulled pork and slaw sliders

the basic

CHICKEN SCHNITZEL

CHICKEN SCHNITZEL

300g sourdough bread, chopped

1 tablespoon finely grated lemon rind

2 tablespoons thyme leaves

¼ cup (35g) plain (all-purpose) flour

sea salt and cracked black pepper

2 eggs

¼ cup (60ml) milk

4 x 200g chicken breast fillets, halved horizontally

vegetable oil, for shallow-frying

STEP 1 Place the sourdough, lemon rind and thyme in a food processor and process into fine crumbs. Transfer to a medium tray.

STEP 2 Place the flour, salt and pepper in a medium bowl and mix to combine.

STEP 3 Place the eggs and milk in a separate medium bowl and whisk to combine.

STEP 4 Using a meat mallet[+], pound the chicken evenly to 5mm thick. Dust each piece of chicken in the flour mixture, dip in the egg mixture and press into the breadcrumb mixture to coat.

STEP 5 Heat 3cm of oil in a large non-stick frying pan over high heat[++]. Cook the chicken in batches, turning, for 3–4 minutes or until golden and cooked through. Drain on paper towel and keep warm[+++]. **SERVES 4**

NOTES

+ If you don't have a meat mallet, you can use a rolling pin or the base of a heavy frying pan to pound the chicken.

++ **To test that the oil is hot enough for frying, drop in a breadcrumb. If it's ready, little bubbles will gather around the crumb.**

+++ To keep the schnitzels warm before serving, place them on a baking tray in an oven preheated to 140°C (275°F).

TIPS

These schnitzels can be crumbed in advance. At the end of step 4, wrap them individually in plastic wrap and freeze. Simply thaw and cook when ready to eat, as per step 5.

Serve schnitzels with lemon wedges.

chicken schnitzel with dill potato salad and crispy capers

chicken schnitzel banh mi

chicken parmigiana

chicken schnitzel with dill potato salad and crispy capers

2 tablespoons extra virgin olive oil
¼ cup (40g) baby capers, rinsed and drained
1 x quantity chicken schnitzel (see *basic recipe*),
   heated through
sea salt and cracked black pepper
lemon wedges, to serve
dill potato salad
800g baby (chat) potatoes, halved
½ cup (150g) mayonnaise
1 teaspoon finely grated lemon rind
¼ cup (60ml) lemon juice
2 stalks celery, finely chopped and leaves reserved
¼ cup chopped dill
¼ cup finely chopped flat-leaf parsley

To make the dill potato salad, place the potato in a medium saucepan and cover with cold water. Bring to the boil over high heat and cook for 15–18 minutes or until just tender. Drain and cool under cold running water. Drain well and allow to cool completely. Place the mayonnaise, lemon rind and lemon juice in a large bowl and mix to combine. Add the potato, celery, reserved celery leaves, dill and parsley and toss to combine.

   Heat the oil in a small non-stick frying pan over high heat. Add the capers and cook for 1 minute or until crisp. Drain on paper towel.

   Divide the schnitzels and salad between serving plates and top with the capers. Sprinkle with salt and pepper and serve with lemon wedges. **SERVES 4**

chicken schnitzel banh mi

¼ cup (60ml) apple cider vinegar
1 tablespoon caster (superfine) sugar
2 carrots, peeled and shredded
2 small red chillies, thinly sliced[+]
1 x quantity chicken schnitzel (see *basic recipe*), sliced
2 Lebanese cucumbers, thinly sliced lengthways
2 x 80cm-long baguettes, tops sliced
chilli sauce and Japanese mayonnaise*, to serve
1 cup coriander (cilantro) leaves

Place the vinegar and sugar in a medium bowl and stir until the sugar has dissolved. Add the carrot and chilli and toss to combine. Set aside to pickle for 10 minutes.

   Divide the schnitzel and cucumber between the baguettes. Top with the pickled carrot and chilli, chilli sauce, mayonnaise and coriander. Slice to serve. **SERVES 8**

NOTE

+ For a milder flavour, halve the chillies lengthways and remove the seeds and membranes before slicing and pickling.

chicken parmigiana

1 x quantity chicken schnitzel (see *basic recipe*)
250g buffalo mozzarella*, torn
250g truss cherry tomatoes, torn
½ x quantity basil pesto (see *basic recipe*, page 211)
   or ½ cup (130g) store-bought basil pesto
1 cup basil leaves

Preheat oven to 250°C (480°F). Place the schnitzels on an oven tray. Top with the mozzarella and tomato. Bake for 6–8 minutes or until the cheese is melted and golden and the schnitzels are heated through. Spoon the pesto over and sprinkle with the basil to serve. **SERVES 4**

STICKY MAPLE AND BOURBON PORK RIBS

STICKY MAPLE AND BOURBON PORK RIBS

2 cups (500ml) malt vinegar

2 litres water

6 bay leaves

3 sticks cinnamon

½ cup (90g) brown sugar

¼ cup (75g) rock salt

1 brown onion, quartered

2kg American-style pork ribs

maple bourbon glaze

1 cup (250ml) bourbon or whiskey

½ cup (125ml) maple syrup

½ cup (125ml) malt vinegar

¼ cup (60ml) Worcestershire sauce

1 tablespoon Dijon mustard

1 teaspoon smoked paprika*

1 tablespoon sea salt flakes

STEP 1 Place the vinegar, water, bay leaves, cinnamon, sugar, rock salt and onion in a large saucepan over high heat. Stir to combine and bring to the boil.

STEP 2 Add the ribs, reduce the heat to medium and cover with a tight-fitting lid. Simmer for 30–40 minutes or until the pork is tender.

STEP 3 While the ribs are cooking, make the maple bourbon glaze. Place the bourbon, maple syrup, vinegar, Worcestershire sauce, mustard, paprika and salt flakes in a medium saucepan over medium heat. Stir to combine and bring to the boil. Reduce the heat to low and simmer for 8–10 minutes or until slightly reduced. Set aside.

STEP 4 Preheat oven to 220°C (425°F).

STEP 5 Remove the ribs from the cooking liquid and place, meat-side down, in a large deep-sided ovenproof dish. Top with the glaze and roast for 15 minutes.

STEP 6 Turn the ribs over, baste with the glaze and roast for a further 15 minutes or until the pork is tender and the glaze is reduced. Brush with any remaining glaze and slice to serve. **SERVES 4**

american-style sticky pork ribs with fennel and apple slaw

maple-glazed pork rolls with watercress and lemon aioli

american-style sticky pork ribs
with fennel and apple slaw

1 x quantity sticky maple and bourbon pork ribs
    (see *basic recipe*), heated through
fennel and apple slaw
¼ cup (75g) mayonnaise
2 tablespoons lemon juice
4 cups (320g) shredded white cabbage
1 medium fennel bulb (300g), trimmed and thinly sliced
2 Granny Smith (green) apples, halved and thinly sliced
2 tablespoons chopped dill

To make the fennel and apple slaw, place the mayonnaise
and lemon juice in a large bowl and mix to combine.
Add the cabbage, fennel, apple and dill and toss to combine.
    Divide the pork ribs and slaw between serving plates
to serve. **SERVES 4**

maple-glazed pork rolls
with watercress and lemon aioli

½ cup (150g) aioli
1 teaspoon finely grated lemon rind
1 x quantity sticky maple and bourbon pork ribs
    (see *basic recipe*)
6 dill pickles, sliced
3 cups (45g) watercress sprigs
6 soft white bread rolls, halved
asian chilli jam (see *basic recipe*, page 132)
    or store-bought chilli jam, to serve

Place the aioli and lemon rind in a small bowl. Mix to
combine and set aside.
    Cut the pork meat from the ribs+, discarding the bones.
Divide the lemon aioli, pork, pickle and watercress between
the bases of the rolls. Spread the top halves of the rolls with
chilli jam and sandwich onto the bases to serve. **MAKES 6**

NOTE
+ The pork will come away from the
bones more easily if it's still warm.

sticky pork ribs with
sweet potato chilli fries

1 x quantity sticky maple and bourbon pork ribs
    (see *basic recipe*), heated through
½ cup (150g) aioli
sweet potato chilli fries
700g orange sweet potatoes (kumara),
    thinly sliced lengthways
700g white sweet potatoes (kumara),
    thinly sliced lengthways
1 teaspoon dried chilli flakes
¼ cup (60ml) extra virgin olive oil
sea salt

To make the sweet potato chilli fries, preheat oven to
220°C (425°F). Place the sweet potato, chilli flakes and oil
in a large bowl and toss well to combine. Divide between
2 large oven trays and roast for 10 minutes. Turn and roast
for a further 5 minutes or until crisp. Sprinkle with salt.
    Divide the pork ribs and chilli fries between serving
plates and serve with the aioli. **SERVES 4**

TIP
This recipe calls for orange and
white sweet potato. You can use
either or both, or try roasting
other thinly sliced root vegetables
like parsnip or beetroot.

sticky pork ribs with sweet potato chilli fries

the basic

CHEESY SOUFFLÉ MIXTURE

CHEESY SOUFFLÉ MIXTURE

30g unsalted butter

¼ cup (35g) plain (all-purpose) flour

⅔ cup (160ml) milk

4 eggs, separated

½ cup (120g) fresh ricotta

½ cup (60g) finely grated gruyere*

½ cup (40g) finely grated parmesan

1 teaspoon Dijon mustard

sea salt and cracked black pepper

1 eggwhite, extra

STEP 1 Melt the butter in a medium saucepan over low heat.

STEP 2 Add the flour and cook, stirring, for 1 minute.

STEP 3 Gradually add the milk and cook, stirring, for 5–8 minutes or until the mixture is thick and glossy.

STEP 4 Remove from the heat. Add the egg yolks, ricotta, gruyere, parmesan, mustard, salt and pepper and mix to combine. Transfer to a large bowl and set aside.

STEP 5 Place the eggwhites and extra eggwhite in the bowl of an electric mixer and whisk until stiff peaks form[+].

MAKES 1 QUANTITY

NOTE
+ See the recipes that follow for how to combine and cook the soufflé mixture.

savoury

114

three-cheese soufflés

spinach and cheese soufflés

smoked trout and chive soufflé

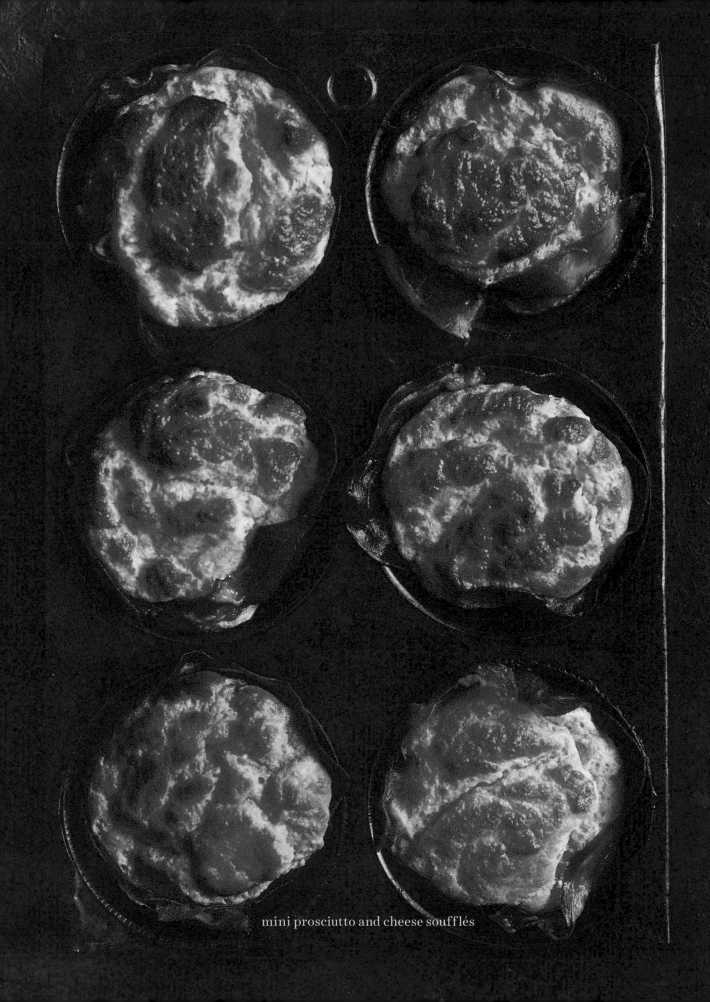

mini prosciutto and cheese soufflés

three-cheese soufflés

melted unsalted butter, for brushing
2 tablespoons finely grated parmesan
1 x quantity cheesy soufflé mixture (see *basic recipe*)

Preheat oven to 200°C (400°F). Brush 2 x 2¼-cup-capacity (560ml) ovenproof dishes with butter and sprinkle with the parmesan. Refrigerate until ready to use.

Add one-third of the soufflé mixture's eggwhite to the cheese mixture and, using a metal spoon, gently fold to combine. Add the remaining eggwhite and gently fold to combine.

Divide the mixture between the prepared dishes, place on a baking tray and bake for 20–25 minutes or until puffed and golden. Serve immediately. **SERVES 4**

spinach and cheese soufflés

melted unsalted butter, for brushing
2 tablespoons finely grated parmesan, plus extra to serve
200g baby spinach leaves
1 x quantity cheesy soufflé mixture (see *basic recipe*)

Preheat oven to 200°C (400°F). Brush 4 x 1½-cup-capacity (375ml) ovenproof ramekins with butter and sprinkle with the parmesan. Refrigerate until ready to use.

Place the spinach in a large heatproof bowl, cover with boiling water and set aside for 1 minute. Drain, place in a clean tea towel, squeeze to remove the excess liquid and finely chop. Add the spinach to the soufflé mixture's cheese mixture and stir to combine. Add one-third of the eggwhite to the spinach mixture and, using a metal spoon, gently fold to combine. Add the remaining eggwhite and gently fold to combine.

Divide the mixture between the prepared ramekins, place on a baking tray and bake for 20–25 minutes or until puffed and golden. Sprinkle with extra parmesan and serve immediately. **MAKES 4**

smoked trout and chive soufflé

200g hot-smoked trout, flaked
¼ cup finely chopped chives
1 x quantity cheesy soufflé mixture (see *basic recipe*)
25g unsalted butter
lemon wedges, to serve

Preheat oven to 200°C (400°F). Add half the trout and half the chives to the soufflé mixture's cheese mixture and stir to combine. Add one-third of the eggwhite to the trout mixture and, using a metal spoon, gently fold to combine. Add the remaining eggwhite and gently fold to combine.

Melt the butter in a 25cm ovenproof non-stick frying pan over medium heat. Remove from the heat, add the soufflé mixture and top with the remaining trout and chives. Transfer to the oven and bake for 12–15 minutes or until puffed and golden. Serve immediately with lemon wedges. **SERVES 4**

mini prosciutto and cheese soufflés

18 slices prosciutto* (270g), halved
1 x quantity cheesy soufflé mixture (see *basic recipe*)

Preheat oven to 200°C (400°F). Lightly grease 12 x ½-cup-capacity (125ml) muffin tins. Line each tin with 3 prosciutto halves. Set aside.

Add one-third of the soufflé mixture's eggwhite to the cheese mixture and, using a metal spoon, gently fold to combine. Add the remaining eggwhite and gently fold to combine.

Divide the mixture between the prepared tins. Bake for 10–12 minutes or until puffed and golden. Serve immediately. **MAKES 12**

TIP
Serve soufflés warm, puffed and golden straight from the oven, with slices of buttered sourdough toast.

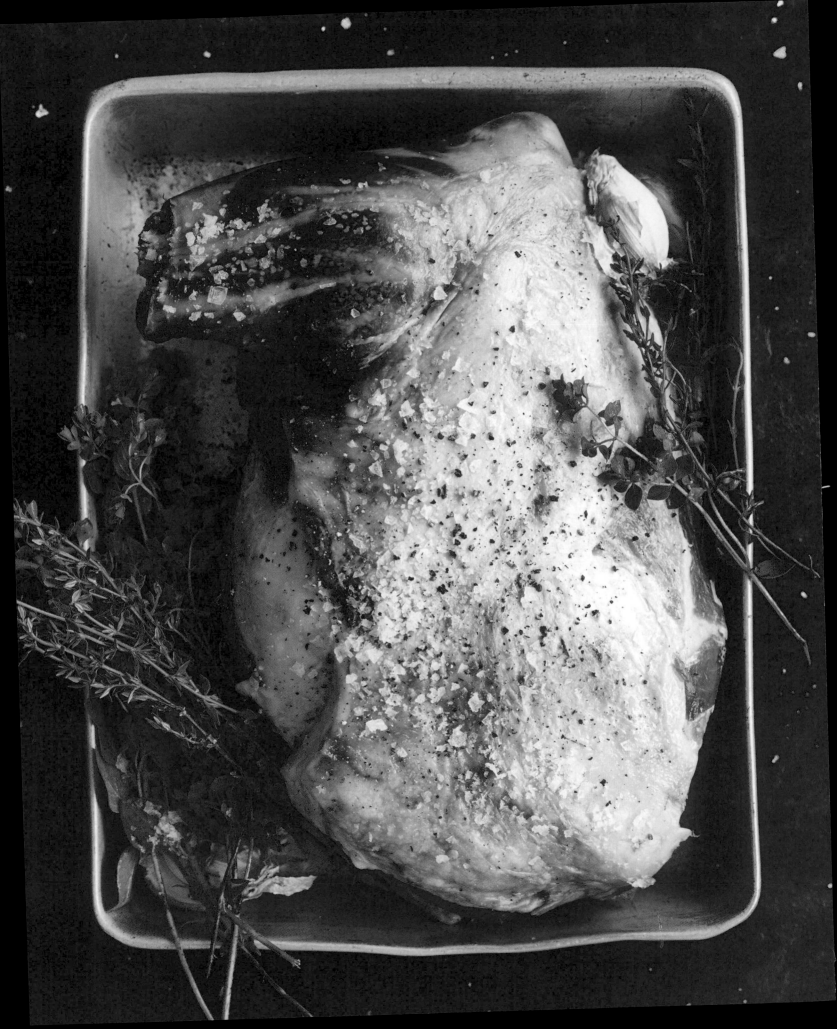

the basic

SLOW-ROASTED LAMB SHOULDER

SLOW-ROASTED LAMB SHOULDER

¼ cup (45g) brown sugar

¼ cup (60ml) malt vinegar

1 bulb garlic, broken into cloves

1 bunch thyme

1 bunch oregano

2 sprigs rosemary

2 cups (500ml) chicken stock

1 x 2kg lamb shoulder, bone in and trimmed

sea salt and cracked black pepper

STEP 1 Preheat oven to 180°C (350°F).

STEP 2 Place the sugar and vinegar in a medium jug and mix to combine. Set aside.

STEP 3 Place the garlic, thyme, oregano and rosemary in the centre of a large roasting pan and add the stock.

STEP 4 Place the lamb, skin-side down, on the garlic and herbs[+]. Sprinkle with salt and pepper. Top with the vinegar mixture and rub to coat. Cover the pan tightly with aluminium foil and roast for 2 hours 30 minutes or until the lamb is tender.

STEP 5 Turn the lamb over and roast, uncovered, for a further 30 minutes or until dark golden.

STEP 6 Brush with the pan juices and shred the meat, discarding the bone, to serve. **SERVES 4**

NOTE
+ Making a 'bed' of garlic and herbs for the lamb gives flavour to the meat and helps prevent it from drying out.

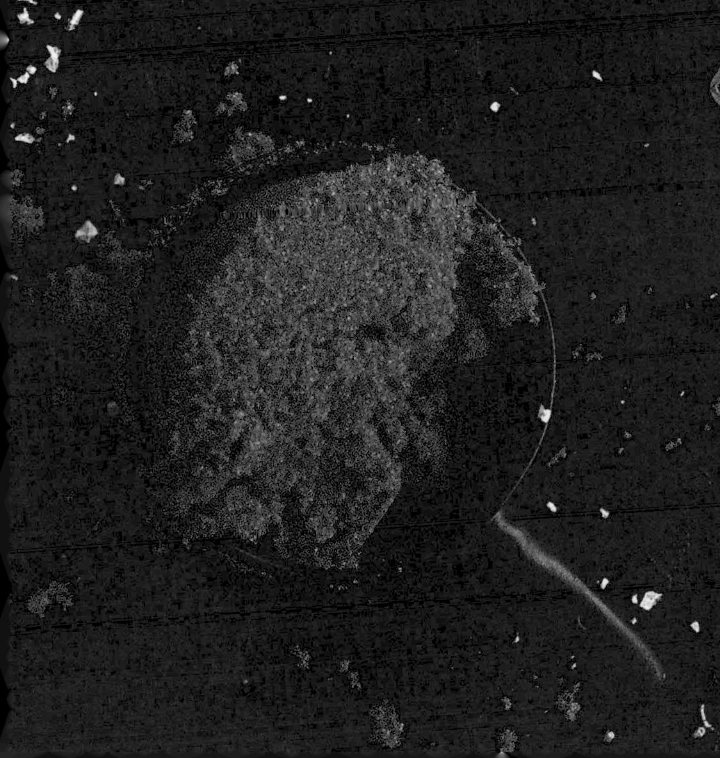

lamb and provolone open sandwiches

5 thick slices crusty white or sourdough bread
2 tablespoons Dijon mustard
2 cups (300g) shredded slow-roasted
   lamb shoulder (see *basic recipe*)
1½ cups (150g) grated provolone*
½ x quantity salsa verde (see *basic recipe*, page 210)
1 cup baby rocket (arugula) leaves

Preheat oven grill (broiler) to high. Place the bread on
an oven tray lined with non-stick baking paper. Grill for
5 minutes or until golden brown. Turn the bread and top
with the mustard, lamb and provolone. Grill for a further
5 minutes or until the cheese is bubbling and golden.
   Spoon the salsa verde over the sandwiches and serve
with the rocket. **MAKES 5**

TIP
Provolone is a mild Italian cow's milk
cheese. You can also use mozzarella,
havarti or your favourite melting cheese
to top these grilled sandwiches.

crispy lamb, pea and mint fritters

1 cup (150g) self-raising (self-rising) flour
1 cup (250ml) milk
2 eggs
1 tablespoon hot English mustard
sea salt and cracked black pepper
2 cups (300g) shredded slow-roasted
   lamb shoulder (see *basic recipe*)
2 cups (80g) finely shredded cavolo nero
   (Tuscan kale)* leaves
1 cup (120g) frozen peas, thawed
½ cup finely chopped chives
¼ cup chopped mint leaves
½ cup (125ml) extra virgin olive oil
lemon wedges, to serve
tomato relish, to serve

Place the flour, milk, eggs, mustard, salt and pepper in
a large bowl and whisk until smooth. Add the lamb, cavolo
nero, peas, chives and mint and mix until just combined.
   Heat a little of the oil in a large non-stick frying pan
over medium heat. In batches, cook ⅓-cups (80ml) of
the mixture for 2–3 minutes each side or until golden
brown and cooked through, adding more oil as necessary.
Serve with lemon wedges and tomato relish. **MAKES 10–12**

TIPS
These golden fritters, made with tender
lamb and packed with greens and herbs,
are perfect for brunch, a simple lunch
or light dinner – kids will love them too.
They're best served hot and crispy from
the pan, but you can keep them warm
in an oven preheated to 140°C (275°F)
while you make the whole batch.

lamb and provolone open sandwiches

crispy lamb, pea and mint fritters

crunchy potato rostis with pulled lamb, yoghurt and mint

lamb, goat's cheese and heirloom tomato salad

crunchy potato rostis with pulled lamb, yoghurt and mint

2 tablespoons malt vinegar
1 tablespoon brown sugar
1 x quantity shredded slow-roasted lamb shoulder
  (see *basic recipe*), heated through
½ cup mint leaves
2 green onions (scallions), thinly sliced
natural Greek-style (thick) yoghurt, to serve
finely grated lemon rind and dried chilli flakes, to serve
crunchy potato rostis
1kg sebago (starchy) potatoes, peeled and grated
½ cup finely chopped chives
2 eggs
sea salt and cracked black pepper
2 tablespoons extra virgin olive oil

To make the crunchy potato rostis, place the potato in a clean tea towel and squeeze to remove the excess liquid[+]. Transfer to a large bowl and add the chives, eggs, salt and pepper and mix well to combine. Heat half the oil in a medium non-stick frying pan over medium heat. Spread half the potato mixture evenly into the pan. Cook for 5 minutes each side or until golden brown and cooked through. Remove from the pan and keep warm. Repeat with the remaining oil and potato mixture.

While the rostis are cooking, place the vinegar and sugar in a large bowl and mix to dissolve the sugar. Add the lamb, mint and onion and toss to coat. Top the rostis with the lamb salad, yoghurt, lemon rind and chilli flakes to serve. **SERVES 4**

NOTE
+ Squeezing the liquid from the potato is an important step – it helps to bind the rostis and ensures the outsides turn golden and extra crispy when cooked.

lamb, goat's cheese and heirloom tomato salad

8 heirloom tomatoes (960g)[+], sliced
½ x quantity shredded slow-roasted lamb shoulder
  (see *basic recipe*)
300g goat's cheese*, crumbled
seeds from 1 pomegranate
1 long green chilli, sliced
½ x quantity salsa verde (see *basic recipe*, page 210)
baby (micro) basil, to serve

Divide the tomato, lamb, goat's cheese, pomegranate and chilli between serving plates. Drizzle with the salsa verde and sprinkle with basil to serve. **SERVES 4**

NOTE
+ Heirloom tomatoes are sweet, flavourful and look beautiful thanks to their varying shapes and colours. Find them at greengrocers and some supermarkets. If unavailable, simply use regular tomatoes.

ASIAN CHILLI JAM

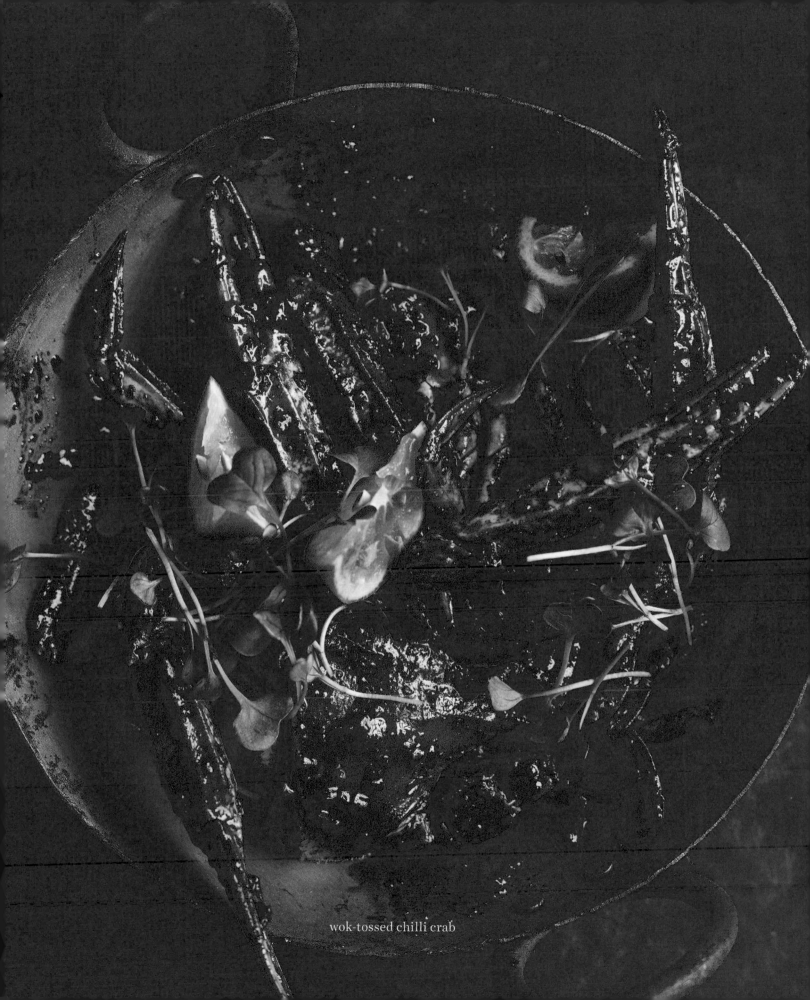

wok-tossed chilli crab

ASIAN CHILLI JAM

5 long red chillies, roughly chopped

1 eschalot (French shallot), roughly chopped

3 cloves garlic, roughly chopped

1 tablespoon chopped ginger

2 tablespoons peanut oil

2 teaspoons sesame oil

¼ cup (60ml) rice wine vinegar

2 tablespoons fish sauce*

⅔ cup (120g) brown sugar

STEP 1 Place the chilli, eschalot, garlic and ginger in a small food processor and process until finely chopped.

STEP 2 Heat the peanut oil and sesame oil in a large non-stick frying pan over medium heat.

STEP 3 Add the chilli mixture and cook, stirring, for 6–8 minutes or until just beginning to caramelise.

STEP 4 Add the vinegar, fish sauce and sugar and stir to combine. Cook for a further 2–3 minutes or until thickened[+].

MAKES ¾ CUP

—

NOTE
+ Chilli jam will thicken further on cooling.
TIP
Keep the chilli jam refrigerated in a sealed jar or airtight container for up to 3 weeks.

quick chilli-grilled fish

wok-tossed chilli crab

2 tablespoons peanut oil
4 x 325g green (uncooked) blue swimmer crabs*,
    quartered and cleaned
1 x quantity Asian chilli jam (see *basic recipe*)
baby (micro) purple radish leaves, to serve
lemon wedges, to serve

Heat the oil in a large wok or non-stick frying pan
over high heat. Add the crab and cook, stirring, for
2 minutes. Add the chilli jam and cook, stirring
occasionally, for a further 6–8 minutes or until the
crab is cooked through. Top with radish leaves and
serve with lemon wedges. **SERVES 4 AS A STARTER OR SIDE**

TIP
*Ask your fishmonger to cut and clean
the crab for you.*

quick chilli-grilled fish

12 small white fish fillets (1kg)[+], skin on and pin-boned
1 x quantity Asian chilli jam (see *basic recipe*)
2 green onions (scallions), thinly sliced
1 cup coriander (cilantro) leaves
lime wedges, to serve

Preheat oven grill (broiler) to high. Place the fish,
skin-side down, on an oven tray lined with non-stick
baking paper. Brush with the chilli jam and grill
for 3–4 minutes or until golden and cooked through.
Top with the onion and coriander and serve with
lime wedges. **SERVES 4**

NOTE
*+ You can use snapper, whiting or your
choice of white fish fillets for this recipe.*

barbecued chilli prawn skewers

24 green (uncooked) prawns (shrimp) (1.2kg), peeled
    and deveined with heads and tails intact
1 x quantity Asian chilli jam (see *basic recipe*)
sliced long red chilli, to serve
Thai basil leaves, to serve
grilled lime halves, to serve

Preheat a char-grill pan or barbecue over high heat.
Thread the prawns onto bamboo skewers and brush
with the chilli jam. Cook, turning, for 4–5 minutes
or until cooked through. Top with chilli and basil and
serve with grilled lime halves. **SERVES 4 AS A STARTER OR SIDE**

barbecued chilli prawn skewers

SIMPLE RISOTTO

SIMPLE RISOTTO

50g unsalted butter

1 onion, finely chopped

2 cloves garlic, thinly sliced

½ cup (125ml) white wine

2 cups (400g) arborio rice
or risotto rice

1.5 litres hot chicken stock

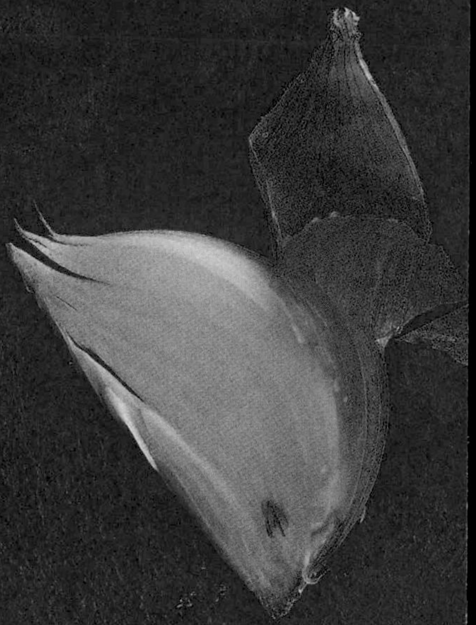

STEP 1 Melt half the butter in a medium saucepan over medium heat.

STEP 2 Add the onion and garlic and cook, stirring occasionally, for 4–5 minutes or until translucent.

STEP 3 Add the wine and cook for 2 minutes.

STEP 4 Add the rice and cook, stirring frequently, for 2 minutes.

STEP 5 Add the stock, 1 cup (250ml) at a time, adding more only once each addition has been absorbed, and cook, stirring frequently, for 20–25 minutes or until the rice is al dente.

STEP 6 Add the remaining butter and stir to combine. **SERVES 4**

spinach risotto with burrata and basil pesto

pea and mint risotto with crispy chorizo

spinach risotto with burrata and basil pesto

100g baby spinach leaves
1 x quantity simple risotto (see *basic recipe*),
    heated through
⅓ cup (90g) basil pesto (see *basic recipe*, page 211)
    or store-bought basil pesto
2 x 200g burrata*, torn
sea salt and cracked black pepper
baby (micro) basil, to serve

Add the spinach to the risotto and stir to combine+.
Divide between serving bowls and top with the
pesto and burrata. Sprinkle with salt, pepper and
basil to serve. **SERVES 4**

NOTE
+ *The spinach will wilt as it's*
stirred through the hot risotto.

pea and mint risotto with crispy chorizo

1 tablespoon extra virgin olive oil
250g air-dried chorizo*, cases removed
    and processed until finely chopped
1½ cups (240g) podded peas+
1 x quantity simple risotto (see *basic recipe*),
    heated through
1 cup mint leaves
½ cup (40g) finely grated parmesan
1 teaspoon finely grated lemon rind

Heat the oil in a large non-stick frying pan over
high heat. Add the chorizo and cook for 4–5 minutes
or until crisp.
    Add the peas to the risotto and stir to combine.
Top with the chorizo, mint, parmesan and lemon
rind to serve. **SERVES 4**

NOTE
+ *You'll need about 620g fresh peas*
in the pod to get the required amount
of podded peas for this recipe. If you
prefer, you can use thawed frozen peas.

lemon and asparagus risotto with maple-glazed pancetta

180g thinly sliced pancetta*
¼ cup (60ml) maple syrup
1 x quantity simple risotto (see *basic recipe*),
    heated through
2 bunches asparagus (150g), trimmed,
    shaved and blanched+
½ cup (40g) finely grated parmesan
1 teaspoon finely grated lemon rind

Preheat oven to 180°C (350°F). Place the pancetta
on a lightly greased oven tray lined with non-stick
baking paper and brush with the maple syrup.
Roast for 10–15 minutes or until crisp.
    Divide the risotto between serving bowls and top
with the pancetta, asparagus, parmesan and lemon
rind to serve. **SERVES 4**

NOTE
+ *Use a vegetable peeler to shave*
the asparagus, working from base
to tip. Alternatively, slice it thinly
lengthways using a sharp knife.

lemon and asparagus risotto with maple-glazed pancetta

the basic

ESSENTIAL MINCE MIXTURE

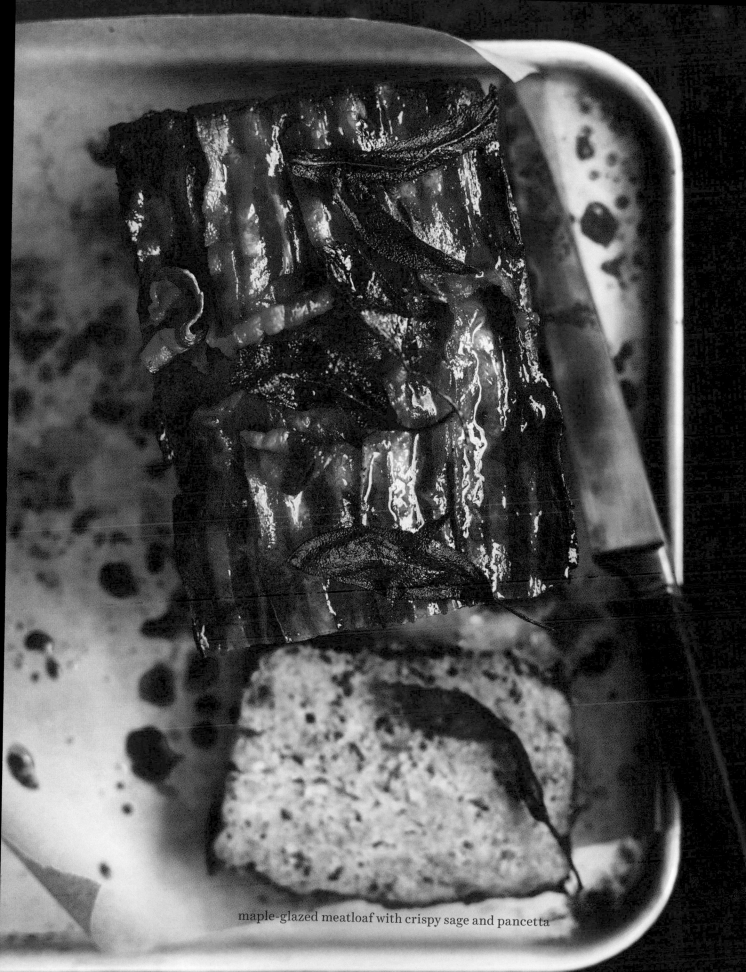

maple-glazed meatloaf with crispy sage and pancetta

ESSENTIAL MINCE MIXTURE

1 cup (70g) fresh breadcrumbs

1/4 cup (60ml) milk

2 teaspoons fennel seeds

2 teaspoons sea salt flakes

1 teaspoon dried chilli flakes

500g pork mince

500g veal mince

1 tablespoon finely grated lemon rind

1 egg yolk

1 cup (80g) finely grated parmesan

2 tablespoons thyme leaves, chopped

4 cloves garlic, crushed

1 tablespoon Dijon mustard

cracked black pepper

STEP 1 Place the breadcrumbs and milk in a large bowl and allow to stand for 5 minutes.

STEP 2 Place the fennel seeds, salt and chilli flakes in a mortar and lightly crush with a pestle.

STEP 3 Add the fennel mixture, pork and veal mince, lemon rind, egg yolk, parmesan, thyme, garlic, mustard and pepper to the breadcrumb mixture and mix for 2–3 minutes or until well combined[+]. **MAKES 1 QUANTITY**

NOTE
+ See the recipes that follow for how to cook this mince mixture.
TIP
You can buy combined pork and veal mince from your butcher.

spaghetti and meatballs

maple-glazed meatloaf with crispy sage and pancetta

200g thinly sliced flat pancetta*
1 x quantity essential mince mixture (see *basic recipe*)
2 tablespoons maple syrup
¼ cup sage leaves

Preheat oven to 180°C (350°F). Lightly grease a 10cm x 20cm (2-litre-capacity) loaf tin. Line the tin with the pancetta, overlapping the slices to cover the base and sides, allowing the excess to hang over the edges. Press the mince mixture into the tin+ and fold in the overhanging pancetta. Place in the oven and cook for 1 hour or until the meatloaf is cooked through and the pancetta is crisp.

Remove the meatloaf from the oven and increase the oven temperature to 200°C (400°F). Allow the meatloaf to cool in the tin for 5 minutes. Remove from the tin and place, top-side up, on a wire rack set over a baking tray. Brush the top and sides of the meatloaf with the maple syrup, sprinkle with the sage leaves and roast for a further 5–8 minutes or until golden and caramelised and the sage is crisp. Slice to serve. **SERVES 4–6**

NOTE
+ *Use the back of a spoon to press the mince mixture firmly into the tin. This will help the meatloaf hold its shape and give it an even texture.*

TIPS
Store meatloaf in an airtight container in the refrigerator for up to 3 days.
To freeze, simply slice the cooked meatloaf and place between sheets of non-stick baking paper in an airtight container in the freezer. You can freeze meatloaf for up to 3 months.

spaghetti and meatballs

1 x quantity essential mince mixture (see *basic recipe*)
¼ cup (60ml) extra virgin olive oil
4 cloves garlic, crushed
1 litre tomato puree (passata)
¼ cup (60ml) chicken stock or water
6 sprigs basil
1 teaspoon caster (superfine) sugar
sea salt and cracked black pepper
500g spaghetti
grated parmesan and extra basil leaves, to serve

Roll heaped tablespoons of the mince mixture into balls. Heat 1 tablespoon of the oil in a large non-stick frying pan over high heat. Cook the meatballs in batches, turning, for 5–6 minutes or until browned. Set aside and keep warm.

Wipe the pan clean with paper towel and reduce the heat to medium. Add the remaining oil and the garlic. Cook, stirring, for 30 seconds. Add the puree, stock, basil, sugar, salt and pepper and bring to a simmer. Return the meatballs to the pan and cook for 8 minutes or until cooked through and the sauce is slightly reduced.

While the sauce and meatballs are cooking, cook the pasta in a large saucepan of salted boiling water for 8–10 minutes or until al dente. Drain and divide between serving plates. Top with the meatballs and sauce, discarding the basil sprigs, and sprinkle with the parmesan and extra basil to serve. **SERVES 4–6**

the best burgers

1 x quantity essential mince mixture (see *basic recipe*)
6 burger buns, halved
½ cup (140g) caramelised onion relish
¼ cup (75g) aioli
50g manchego*, thinly sliced
4 dill pickles (240g), sliced
½ cup rocket (arugula) leaves

Preheat a char-grill pan or barbecue over medium heat. Divide the mince mixture into 6 portions and shape into 10cm round patties. Cook the patties for 5 minutes each side or until browned and cooked through. Set aside.

Toast the cut sides of the burger buns for 30 seconds or until just charred. Divide the relish and aioli between the bun bases. Top with the manchego, patties, pickle and rocket. Sandwich with the tops of the buns to serve. **MAKES 6**

the best burgers

the basic

———

SALT AND PEPPER SPICE MIX

salt and pepper squid

SALT AND PEPPER SPICE MIX

1 tablespoon Sichuan peppercorns*

1 teaspoon dried chilli flakes

1½ teaspoons Chinese five-spice powder*

2 teaspoons sea salt flakes

STEP 1 Heat a small non-stick frying pan over medium heat. Add the peppercorns, chilli flakes, five-spice powder and salt and cook, stirring, for 1 minute or until fragrant.

STEP 2 Transfer to a small food processor and process into a coarse powder[+]. **MAKES 1 QUANTITY**

NOTE
+ See the recipes that follow for how to use this spice mix.
TIP
Toasting the mix before grinding it helps to bring out the flavours and aromas of the spices.

crispy salt and pepper prawns with fried chilli

salt and pepper squid

vegetable oil, for deep-frying
½ cup (90g) white rice flour
1 x quantity salt and pepper spice mix (see *basic recipe*)
10 small squid hoods* (1.8kg), cleaned, quartered and scored
2 eggwhites, lightly beaten
lemon wedges, to serve

Fill a large saucepan half-full with oil and place over medium heat until the temperature reaches 180°C (350°F) on a deep-frying thermometer.

While the oil is heating, place the flour in a large bowl. Add 1 tablespoon of the salt and pepper spice mix and stir to combine, reserving the remaining spice mix. Dip the squid in the eggwhite and toss in the flour mixture to coat.

Deep-fry the squid, in batches, for 1 minute or until crisp. Drain on paper towel.

Place the squid on a serving plate and sprinkle with the reserved salt and pepper spice mix. Toss to coat and serve with lemon wedges. **SERVES 4 AS A STARTER OR SIDE**

crispy salt and pepper prawns with fried chilli

vegetable oil, for deep-frying
½ cup (90g) white rice flour
1 x quantity salt and pepper spice mix (see *basic recipe*)
24 green (uncooked) king prawns (shrimp) (1.2kg),
   peeled and deveined with tails intact
2 eggwhites, lightly beaten
4 long red chillies, finely shredded
lime wedges, to serve

Fill a large saucepan half-full with oil and place over medium heat until the temperature reaches 180°C (350°F) on a deep-frying thermometer.

While the oil is heating, place the flour in a large bowl. Add 1 tablespoon of the salt and pepper spice mix and stir to combine, reserving the remaining spice mix. Dip the prawns in the eggwhite and toss in the flour mixture to coat.

Deep-fry the prawns, in batches, for 1–2 minutes or until crisp and cooked through. Drain on paper towel. Deep-fry the chilli for 2–3 minutes or until crisp. Drain on paper towel.

Place the prawns in a serving bowl and sprinkle with the reserved salt and pepper spice mix. Toss to coat and serve with the chilli and lime wedges. **SERVES 4 AS A STARTER OR SIDE**

asian-style salt and pepper chicken with green mango salad

2 tablespoons vegetable oil
4 x 180g chicken breast fillets, trimmed
   and thickly sliced
1 x quantity salt and pepper spice mix (see *basic recipe*)
baby (micro) shiso, to serve
lime wedges, to serve
green mango salad
2 tablespoons lime juice
1 tablespoon fish sauce*
1 tablespoon brown sugar
1 green mango*, peeled and shredded
1 long green chilli, shredded
1 cup coriander (cilantro) leaves

To make the green mango salad, place the lime juice, fish sauce and sugar in a large bowl and mix until the sugar has dissolved. Add the mango, chilli and coriander. Toss to combine and set aside.

Heat half the oil in a large non-stick frying pan over high heat. Add half the chicken and cook for 2–3 minutes each side or until just golden. Sprinkle the chicken with half the salt and pepper spice mix and cook for a further 1 minute each side or until well-coated, golden brown and cooked through. Set aside and keep warm. Wipe the pan out with paper towel and repeat with the remaining oil, chicken and spice mix.

Divide the chicken and green mango salad between serving plates. Top with shiso and serve with lime wedges. **SERVES 4**

TIP
Find green mangoes at Asian grocers and greengrocers. If unavailable, try using green papaya instead.

asian-style salt and pepper chicken with green mango salad

the basic

FRITTATA MIXTURE

FRITTATA MIXTURE

6 eggs

1 cup (250ml) single (pouring) cream*

⅓ cup (25g) finely grated parmesan

sea salt and cracked black pepper

STEP 1 Place the eggs, cream, parmesan, salt
and pepper in a large bowl and whisk to combine+.

MAKES 1 QUANTITY

——

NOTE
+ *See the recipes that follow for
how to cook this frittata mixture.*
TIP
*Use fresh, room temperature
eggs when possible – they'll make
for a lighter, puffier frittata.*

simple cheese frittata

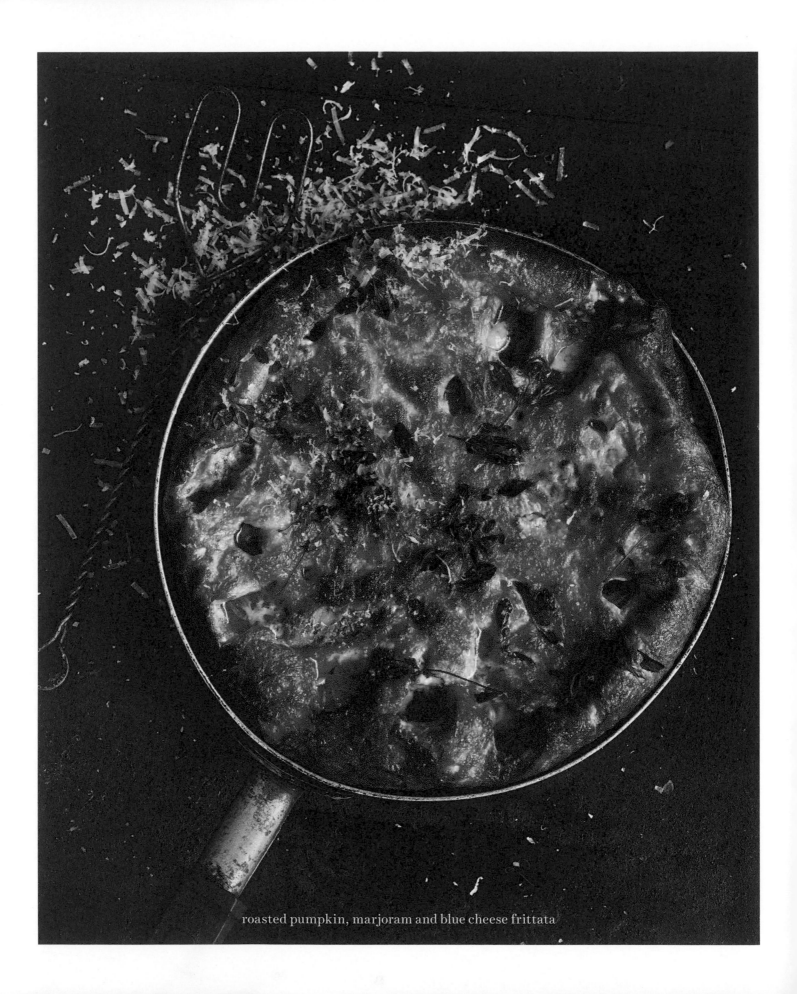

roasted pumpkin, marjoram and blue cheese frittata

pancetta and sage mini frittatas

simple cheese frittata

1 teaspoon extra virgin olive oil
20g unsalted butter
1 x quantity frittata mixture (see *basic recipe*)
½ cup (60g) grated cheddar
1½ cups (360g) fresh ricotta, crumbled
finely grated parmesan, to serve

Preheat oven to 200°C (400°F). Heat a 22cm ovenproof
non-stick frying pan over low heat. Add the oil and butter
and swirl to cover the base and edges of the pan. Add the
frittata mixture and cook for 5 minutes or until the edges
begin to set. Top with the cheddar and ricotta and cook
for a further 15 minutes. Transfer to the oven and bake
for 10–12 minutes or until the frittata is golden and just
set. Sprinkle with parmesan and slice to serve. **SERVES 4**

roasted pumpkin, marjoram and blue cheese frittata

300g butternut pumpkin, peeled and cut into 2cm cubes
1 tablespoon extra virgin olive oil
sea salt and cracked black pepper
1 teaspoon extra virgin olive oil, extra
20g unsalted butter
1 x quantity frittata mixture (see *basic recipe*)
½ cup marjoram* leaves
½ cup (60g) grated cheddar
100g blue cheese, crumbled
finely grated parmesan, to serve

Preheat oven to 200°C (400°F). Place the pumpkin in a
bowl and add the oil, salt and pepper. Toss to combine and
transfer to a lightly greased oven tray lined with non-stick
baking paper. Roast for 12–15 minutes or until golden.
  Heat a 22cm ovenproof non-stick frying pan over low
heat. Add the extra oil and the butter and swirl to cover
base and edges of the pan. Add the frittata mixture and
cook for 5 minutes or until the edges begin to set. Top
with the pumpkin, marjoram, cheddar and blue cheese
and cook for a further 15 minutes. Transfer to the oven
and bake for 8–10 minutes or until the frittata is just set.
Sprinkle with parmesan and slice to serve. **SERVES 4**

pancetta and sage mini frittatas

18 thin slices round pancetta* (180g)
1 x quantity frittata mixture (see *basic recipe*)
1 cup (240g) fresh ricotta, crumbled
¼ cup sage leaves
finely grated parmesan, to serve

Preheat oven to 160°C (325°F). Lightly grease
6 x ¾-cup-capacity (180ml) Texas muffin tins.
Line each tin with 3 pancetta slices, allowing 1cm
of pancetta to sit above the edges. Divide the frittata
mixture between the tins and top with the ricotta
and sage. Bake for 35–40 minutes or until golden
and just set. Remove from the tins and sprinkle
with parmesan to serve. **MAKES 6**

kale, thyme and goat's cheese frittata

1 teaspoon extra virgin olive oil
20g unsalted butter
3 cups (90g) shredded kale leaves
1 tablespoon thyme leaves, plus extra sprigs to serve
1 teaspoon finely grated lemon rind
1 x quantity frittata mixture (see *basic recipe*)
½ cup (60g) grated cheddar
150g goat's cheese*, crumbled
finely grated parmesan, to serve

Preheat oven to 200°C (400°F). Heat a 22cm ovenproof
non-stick frying pan over low heat. Add the oil and butter
and swirl to cover the base and edges of the pan. Add the
kale and cook for 2–3 minutes or until wilted. Add the
thyme, lemon rind and frittata mixture and cook for
5 minutes or until the edges begin to set. Top with the
cheddar and goat's cheese and cook for a further 15 minutes.
Top with the thyme sprigs, transfer to the oven and bake
for 8–10 minutes or until the frittata is just set. Sprinkle
with parmesan and slice to serve. **SERVES 4**

kale, thyme and goat's cheese frittata

the basic

—

CHINESE BARBECUED DUCK

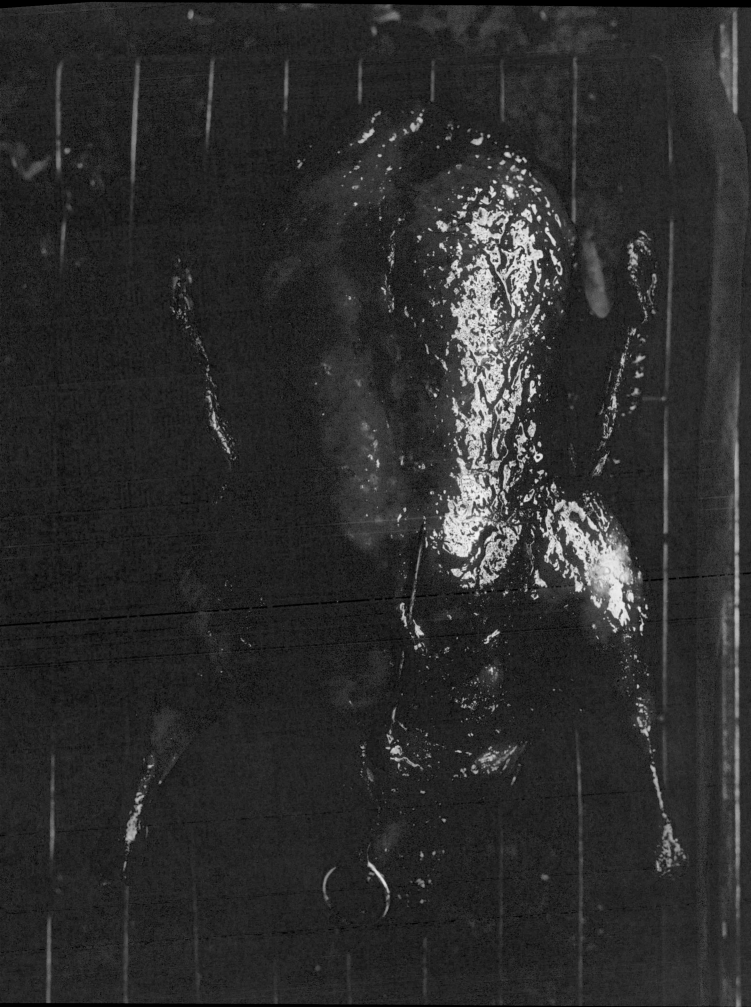

CHINESE BARBECUED DUCK

1 x 2kg whole duck, neck and wing tips removed[+]

1 orange, quartered

50g ginger, sliced

1 green onion (scallion), chopped

5 cloves garlic, bruised

2 star anise

2 sticks cinnamon

2 tablespoons extra virgin olive oil

1 tablespoon sea salt flakes

glaze

2 tablespoons honey

¼ cup (60ml) rice wine vinegar

2 tablespoons char siu sauce*

2 tablespoons Chinese cooking wine (Shaoxing)*

STEP 1 Remove and discard excess fat from the duck cavity.

STEP 2 Place the duck in a large heatproof bowl and pierce the skin, using a skewer. Cover with boiling water and allow to stand for 1 minute, turning halfway. Drain, transfer to a tray and pat dry, using paper towel[++].

STEP 3 Fill the duck cavity with the orange, ginger, onion, garlic, star anise and cinnamon. Fold the skin over the cavity to enclose and use a metal skewer to fasten. Refrigerate for 2–3 hours or until the skin is dry.

STEP 4 Preheat oven to 180°C (350°F).

STEP 5 To make the glaze, place the honey, vinegar, char siu sauce and cooking wine in a small saucepan over medium heat and stir to combine. Bring to the boil, reduce the heat to low and simmer for 3–4 minutes. Set aside to cool slightly.

STEP 6 Rub the duck with the oil and salt and place on a large lightly greased rack set over a roasting pan lined with non-stick baking paper. Roast for 1 hour or until dark golden and cooked through, brushing with the glaze every 10 minutes for the last 30–40 minutes of cooking time[+++].

STEP 7 Allow to cool slightly and slice to serve. **SERVES 4**

NOTES
+ Ask your butcher to trim the wing tips and remove the neck for you, leaving some extra skin to fold over and cover the cavity.
*++ **The duck can be prepared up until the end of step 2, up to 2 days before filling and roasting.***
+++ If you find that parts of the duck are roasting too quickly, simply cover them with aluminium foil.

barbecued duck pancakes

duck, green mango and basil salad

barbecued duck pancakes

16 store-bought Chinese pancakes*, warmed according
   to packet instructions
½ cup (125ml) hoisin sauce*
4 baby cucumbers (cukes) (200g), thinly sliced
2 green onions (scallions), shredded
1 x quantity Chinese barbecued duck (see *basic recipe*),
   heated through and sliced

Spread each pancake with 1 teaspoon of the hoisin
sauce. Top with the cucumber, onion and duck.
Roll to enclose to serve. **SERVES 4**

duck, green mango and basil salad

6 cups (540g) finely shredded Chinese cabbage (wombok)
2 cups (160g) bean sprouts
2 green onions (scallions), shredded
1 green mango*, peeled and shredded
1 cup Thai basil leaves
½ cup (70g) roasted peanuts, chopped
1 long red chilli, shredded
1 cup snow pea (mange tout) tendrils
1 x quantity Chinese barbecued duck (see *basic recipe*),
   thinly sliced
dressing
¼ cup (60ml) lime juice
1 teaspoon sesame oil
1 tablespoon brown sugar
1 tablespoon fish sauce*

To make the dressing, place the lime juice, oil, sugar and
fish sauce in a small bowl and whisk until the sugar has
dissolved. Set aside.

Place the cabbage, bean sprouts, onion, mango and basil
in a large bowl and toss to combine. Divide between serving
bowls and top with the peanuts, chilli, snow pea tendrils
and duck. Drizzle with the dressing to serve. **SERVES 4**

asian noodle stir-fry with barbecued duck and greens

400g dried egg noodles
1 tablespoon sesame oil
1 bunch baby bok choy* (300g), trimmed and halved
2 bunches broccolini (tenderstem)* (350g),
   trimmed and halved
2 green onions (scallions), cut into 5cm lengths
1 x quantity Chinese barbecued duck (see *basic recipe*),
   heated through and sliced
1 cup coriander (cilantro) leaves
½ cup (80g) roasted cashews, chopped
ginger sauce
½ cup (125ml) oyster sauce*
½ cup (125ml) water
2 tablespoons sesame oil
2 tablespoons finely shredded ginger
2 cloves garlic, crushed
½ teaspoon Chinese five-spice powder*

To make the ginger sauce, place the oyster sauce, water,
oil, ginger, garlic and five-spice in a medium bowl and
mix to combine. Set aside.

Cook the noodles according to packet instructions.
Drain and cool under cold running water. Drain well
and set aside.

Heat the oil in a large non-stick frying pan or wok over
high heat. In batches, add the bok choy, broccolini and
onion. Cook, stirring, for 2–3 minutes or until the
bok choy is just wilted. Remove the greens from the pan,
set aside and keep warm.

Add the ginger sauce to the pan and cook for 30 seconds
or until reduced and sticky. Add the noodles and cook,
tossing to coat, for 2–3 minutes or until heated through.
Top with the greens, duck, coriander and cashews to
serve. **SERVES 4**

TIP
*You can use your favourite type of Asian-style
noodles in this fragrant, flavourful stir-fry.*

asian noodle stir-fry with barbecued duck and greens

the basic

MADRAS
CURRY PASTE

MADRAS CURRY PASTE

1 tablespoon mustard seeds

2 tablespoons coriander seeds

2 teaspoons cumin seeds

1 tablespoon smoked paprika*

2 long red chillies, roughly chopped

3 cloves garlic

30g ginger, peeled and sliced

1 tablespoon malt vinegar

1 tablespoon vegetable oil

STEP 1 Heat a small non-stick frying pan over medium heat. Add the mustard, coriander and cumin seeds and toast, shaking the pan frequently, for 2–3 minutes or until fragrant and light golden.

STEP 2 Transfer the seeds to a small food processor and process until ground.

STEP 3 Add the paprika, chilli, garlic, ginger, vinegar and oil and process, scraping down the sides of the bowl, until smooth. **MAKES 1 QUANTITY**

TIPS
Toasting the whole spices before grinding them brings out their full flavours and deep aromas.
Store this curry paste in an airtight container or jar in the refrigerator for up to 2 weeks.

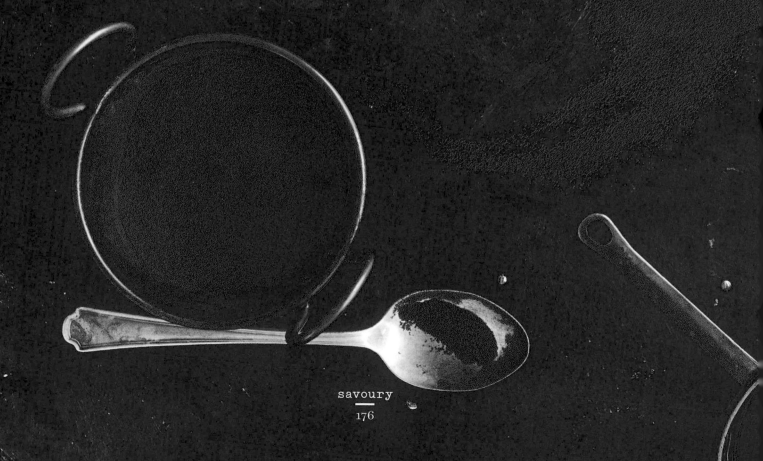

slow-cooked beef madras

indian-style chicken curry with yoghurt and lime pickle

slow-cooked beef madras

1 x quantity madras curry paste (see *basic recipe*)
¼ cup (70g) tomato paste
2 x 400g cans chopped tomatoes
3 cups (750ml) chicken stock
1kg beef blade steak
¼ cup (60ml) apple cider vinegar
1 tablespoon caster (superfine) sugar
2 Lebanese cucumbers, thinly sliced
1 cup coriander (cilantro) leaves
12 pappadums*, cooked according to packet instructions

Preheat oven to 180°C (350°F). Place the curry paste, tomato paste, tomatoes and stock in a large ovenproof heavy-based saucepan and stir to combine. Add the beef and cover with a tight-fitting lid. Place in the oven and cook for 3 hours or until the beef is tender.

Place the vinegar and sugar in a medium bowl and stir until the sugar has dissolved. Add the cucumber, toss to combine and set aside to pickle for 10 minutes.

Remove the beef from the sauce and place on a tray. Using 2 forks, shred the meat. Return the beef to the sauce and stir to combine. Top with the coriander and cucumber and serve with the pappadums. **SERVES 4**

indian-style chicken curry with yoghurt and lime pickle

1 x quantity madras curry paste (see *basic recipe*)
¼ cup (70g) tomato paste
2 x 400g cans chopped tomatoes
3 cups (750ml) chicken stock
1 x 1.6kg whole chicken, skin removed and
   cut into 8 pieces
1 x quantity white rice (see *basic recipe*, page 216)
1 cup coriander (cilantro) leaves
1 cup (280g) natural Greek-style (thick) yoghurt
½ cup (130g) store-bought lime pickle*

Preheat oven to 180°C (350°F). Place the curry paste, tomato paste, tomatoes and stock in a large ovenproof heavy-based saucepan and stir to combine. Add the chicken, place in the oven and cook for 1 hour 30 minutes or until the chicken is cooked through.

Divide the rice and curry between serving bowls and top with the coriander. Serve with the yoghurt and lime pickle. **SERVES 4**

lamb shank madras with pea eggplants, cashews and mint

1 x quantity madras curry paste (see *basic recipe*)
¼ cup (70g) tomato paste
2 x 400g cans chopped tomatoes
3 cups (750ml) chicken stock
6 x 300g lamb shanks, trimmed
150g pea eggplants (aubergines)*
½ cup (80g) roasted cashews, chopped
1 cup mint leaves
1 lemon, cut into wedges

Preheat oven to 180°C (350°F). Place the curry paste, tomato paste, tomatoes and stock in a large ovenproof heavy-based saucepan and stir to combine. Add the lamb shanks and cover with a tight-fitting lid. Place in the oven and cook for 2 hours or until the lamb is tender. Add the eggplants and cook for a further 5 minutes.

Divide the curry between serving bowls and top with the cashew and mint. Serve with lemon wedges. **SERVES 4**

TIP
Serve these fragrant Indian-style curries with steamed basmati rice.

lamb shank madras with pea eggplants, cashews and mint

the basic

CRISPY-SKINNED SALMON

crispy-skinned salmon with parsnip puree and caper brown butter

CRISPY-SKINNED SALMON

1 tablespoon extra virgin olive oil

4 x 150g salmon fillets, skin on

sea salt flakes

STEP 1 Heat half the oil in a large non-stick frying pan over medium heat.

STEP 2 Pat the salmon dry with paper towel and rub the remaining oil and salt into the skin.

STEP 3 Add the salmon to the pan, skin-side down, and top with a heavy-based frying pan or plate to weigh it down[+]. Cook for 4 minutes or until the skin is golden brown and crisp.

STEP 4 Turn and cook, without the weight, for a further 1–2 minutes or until just cooked through. **SERVES 4**

NOTE
+ *Placing a heavy frying pan or plate on top of the salmon helps to keep the skin in contact with the hot pan and ensures it cooks evenly.*

salmon niçoise with green olive dressing

crispy-skinned salmon with cucumber, radish and chervil salad

crispy-skinned salmon with parsnip puree and caper brown butter

1kg parsnips, peeled, trimmed and chopped
100g unsalted butter
¼ cup (50g) baby capers, rinsed and drained
2 tablespoons lemon juice
½ cup (125ml) single (pouring) cream*
sea salt and cracked black pepper
1 x quantity crispy-skinned salmon (see *basic recipe*), still warm

Place the parsnip in a medium saucepan, cover with cold water and place over high heat. Cover with a tight-fitting lid and bring to the boil. Reduce the heat to medium and cook for 5–8 minutes or until very soft.

While the parsnip is cooking, melt the butter in a small non-stick frying pan over high heat. Add the capers and cook, stirring occasionally, for 3–4 minutes or until the butter is just beginning to brown and the capers are crisp. Remove from the heat, add the lemon juice and stir to combine.

Drain the parsnip and return to the saucepan. Add the cream, salt and pepper and, using a hand-held stick blender, blend until smooth.

Place the salmon on a serving plate and top with the caper brown butter. Serve with the parsnip puree. **SERVES 4**

salmon niçoise with green olive dressing

250g green beans, trimmed, blanched and sliced
1 Lebanese cucumber, thinly sliced
1 red onion, thinly sliced
250g mixed cherry tomatoes, halved
1 butter lettuce, trimmed and leaves separated
1 x quantity crispy-skinned salmon (see *basic recipe*), still warm
basil leaves, to serve
green olive dressing
¼ cup (60ml) extra virgin olive oil
2 tablespoons white balsamic vinegar
2 anchovy fillets, finely chopped
1 clove garlic, crushed
1 tablespoon baby capers, rinsed, drained and finely chopped
1 teaspoon Dijon mustard
¾ cup (135g) green (Sicilian) olives, pitted and torn
sea salt and cracked black pepper

To make the green olive dressing, place the oil, vinegar, anchovy, garlic, capers, mustard, olive, salt and pepper in a medium bowl and mix to combine.

Place the beans, cucumber, onion, tomato and half the dressing in a large bowl and toss to combine. Divide the lettuce, salad mixture and salmon between serving plates. Top with basil and drizzle with the remaining dressing to serve. **SERVES 4**

crispy-skinned salmon with cucumber, radish and chervil salad

5 baby cucumbers (cukes) (250g), thinly sliced
4 radishes, trimmed and thinly sliced
2 green onions (scallions), shredded
½ cup chervil* sprigs
¼ cup baby (micro) mint
1 x quantity crispy-skinned salmon (see *basic recipe*), still warm
dressing
¼ cup (60ml) extra virgin olive oil
1 tablespoon lemon juice
½ teaspoon finely grated lemon rind
sea salt and cracked black pepper

To make the dressing, place the oil, lemon juice, lemon rind, salt and pepper in a small bowl and whisk to combine.

Place the cucumber, radish, onion, chervil, mint and the dressing in a large bowl and toss to combine. Divide between serving plates with the salmon to serve. **SERVES 4**

the basic

CLASSIC CHICKEN SOUP BASE

CLASSIC CHICKEN SOUP BASE

1 tablespoon extra virgin olive oil

1 brown onion, chopped

4 cloves garlic, chopped

2 carrots, peeled and chopped

2 stalks celery, trimmed and chopped

200g thinly sliced flat pancetta*, chopped

1 x 1.6kg whole chicken

8 sprigs thyme

1 sprig rosemary

2 fresh bay leaves

3 litres water

STEP 1 Heat the oil in a large saucepan over high heat. Add the onion, garlic, carrot, celery and pancetta. Cook, stirring, for 6–8 minutes or until the vegetables are just tender.

STEP 2 Add the chicken, thyme, rosemary, bay leaves and water and bring to the boil. Reduce the heat to medium, cover with a tight-fitting lid and simmer for 1 hour 30 minutes.

STEP 3 Remove the chicken from the stock and allow to cool slightly. Shred the chicken, discarding the skin and bones, and set aside.

STEP 4 Strain the stock into a large heatproof bowl, discarding the solids. Allow to cool. Skim any excess fat from the surface. **MAKES 1 QUANTITY**

TIPS

You can freeze the chicken stock in airtight containers for up to 3 months. Thaw it to use in soups, sauces, risottos and curries.
Use the tender shredded chicken in anything from soups to sandwiches.

italian-style chicken, cavolo nero and butter bean soup

creamy chicken and corn chowder

italian-style chicken, cavolo nero and butter bean soup

1 x quantity classic chicken soup base (see *basic recipe*)
2 x 400g cans butter beans*, rinsed and drained
1 bunch (220g) cavolo nero (Tuscan kale)*, trimmed
   and leaves shredded
sea salt and cracked black pepper
⅓ cup (90g) basil pesto (see *basic recipe*, page 211)
   or store-bought basil pesto
baby (micro) basil, to serve

Place the chicken stock in a large saucepan over high
heat and bring to the boil. Add the shredded chicken and
the beans and cook for 3 minutes or until heated through.
Add the cavolo nero, salt and pepper and stir to combine.
   Divide between serving bowls, top with the pesto and
sprinkle with basil to serve. **SERVES 4**

creamy chicken and corn chowder

40g unsalted butter
¼ cup (35g) plain (all-purpose) flour
1 x quantity classic chicken soup base (see *basic recipe*)
2 medium sebago (starchy) potatoes, peeled and diced
3 cobs corn, kernels removed
½ cup (125ml) single (pouring) cream*
sea salt and cracked black pepper
finely chopped chives, to serve

Melt the butter in a large saucepan over low heat. Add
the flour and cook, stirring, for 2 minutes. Gradually add
the chicken stock, stirring to combine. Add the potato
and bring to the boil. Add the corn kernels and cook for
5 minutes or until the potato and corn are cooked through.
Add the shredded chicken and cook for 2 minutes or until
heated through. Add the cream and stir to combine.
   Divide between serving bowls and sprinkle with salt,
pepper and chives to serve. **SERVES 4**

chicken noodle soup

1 x quantity classic chicken soup base (see *basic recipe*)
2 baby fennel bulbs, thinly sliced and fronds reserved
200g fresh pappardelle, cut into 5cm lengths
1 medium zucchini (courgette), thinly sliced
sea salt and cracked black pepper
¼ cup finely chopped flat-leaf parsley leaves
¼ cup (20g) finely grated parmesan

Place the chicken stock in a large saucepan over high
heat and bring to the boil. Add the shredded chicken and
fennel and cook for 3 minutes or until the fennel is tender
and the chicken is heated through. Add the pasta and cook,
stirring occasionally, for 3 minutes or until al dente.
Add the zucchini, salt and pepper and stir to combine.
   Divide between serving bowls and top with the parsley,
parmesan and reserved fennel fronds to serve. **SERVES 4**

TIP
*Find fresh pappardelle in the chilled section of
the supermarket, or use your favourite variety
of fresh pasta for this nourishing winter classic.*

chicken noodle soup

the basic
SIMPLE SPELT LOAF

SIMPLE SPELT LOAF

2½ cups (625ml) warm water

1 tablespoon honey

1 teaspoon dry yeast

7 cups (910g) white spelt flour

3 teaspoons sea salt flakes

½ cup (125ml) extra virgin olive oil

STEP 1 Place the water, honey and yeast in a medium jug, mix to combine and set aside.

STEP 2 Place the flour and salt in the bowl of an electric mixer with the dough hook attached. Kneading on low speed, gradually add the yeast mixture and the oil. Knead for 10 minutes or until the dough is smooth.

STEP 3 Transfer the dough to a large lightly greased bowl and cover with plastic wrap. Set aside in a warm place for 1 hour 30 minutes – 2 hours or until the dough has doubled in size.

STEP 4 Preheat oven to 250°C (480°F). Heat a medium ovenproof heavy-based saucepan and tight-fitting lid in the oven for 30 minutes.

STEP 5 Lightly dust the hot pan with flour. Lightly dust a clean surface with flour and turn the dough out. Shape into a round and, using floured hands, carefully place the dough into the saucepan. Dust with flour and, using a small sharp knife, score the top of the dough. Cover with the lid and bake for 30 minutes.

STEP 6 Reduce the oven temperature to 220°C (425°F). Uncover and bake the loaf for a further 20 minutes or until golden and the bread sounds hollow when tapped. **MAKES 1**

TIPS
Spelt flour lends breads and baked goods a lovely earthy nuttiness and golden colour. **It's not gluten free, but some do find it easier to tolerate than wheat flour.**

pumpkin and feta calzone

classic margherita pizza

rustic olive, onion and rosemary flatbread

pumpkin and feta calzone

1kg butternut pumpkin, peeled and chopped into 2cm cubes
1 teaspoon sea salt flakes, plus extra for sprinkling
½ teaspoon cracked black pepper, plus extra for sprinkling
2½ tablespoons extra virgin olive oil, plus extra for drizzling
1 medium garlic bulb, halved horizontally
white spelt flour, for dusting
½ x quantity simple spelt loaf dough (see *basic recipe*)+
150g marinated feta, drained and crumbled
3 marinated artichoke hearts*, drained and quartered
¼ cup marjoram* leaves
1 egg, lightly beaten
1 teaspoon black sesame seeds++

Preheat oven to 220°C (425°F). Place the pumpkin, salt, pepper and 2 tablespoons of the oil in a bowl and toss to coat. Transfer to a lightly greased oven tray lined with non-stick baking paper. Place the garlic, cut-side up, on a sheet of aluminium foil. Drizzle with the remaining oil and sprinkle with extra salt and pepper. Wrap to enclose and place on the oven tray. Roast the pumpkin and garlic for 30 minutes or until the pumpkin is golden brown and the garlic is soft. Allow to cool slightly.

Lightly dust a clean surface with flour and divide the dough in half. Roll each piece out between sheets of non-stick baking paper into a 30cm round. Transfer to 2 lightly greased baking trays and set aside in a warm place for 15 minutes.

Squeeze the garlic cloves from their skins into a bowl and mash. Remove the top sheets of baking paper from the dough and spread each base with garlic. Leaving a 2cm border, top half of each base with the pumpkin, feta, artichoke and marjoram. Brush the edges with the egg and fold the dough over to enclose, pressing and pinching the edges to seal. Brush the calzones with the remaining egg. Drizzle with extra oil and sprinkle with extra salt and the sesame seeds. Bake for 12–15 minutes or until crisp. Slice and serve warm. **MAKES 2**

NOTES
+ This recipe begins with spelt dough – simply prepare the basic recipe until the end of step 3.
++ If you can't find black sesame seeds, you can just use regular white sesame seeds.

classic margherita pizza

white spelt flour, for dusting
½ x quantity simple spelt loaf dough (see *basic recipe*)+
600g fresh mozzarella or bocconcini*, drained and torn
600g cherry tomatoes, squashed and torn
½ cup oregano leaves
extra virgin olive oil, for drizzling
¾ cup (60g) finely grated parmesan
½ cup basil leaves

Preheat oven to 220°C (425°F). Heat a 30cm pizza tray in the oven. Lightly dust a clean surface with flour. Divide the dough into quarters. Roll each piece out into a thin 28cm round. Place 1 round on the hot tray and, working quickly, sprinkle with one-quarter of the mozzarella, tomato and oregano. Drizzle with oil and bake for 12–15 minutes or until the base is crisp and the cheese is golden. Repeat with the remaining bases and toppings. Sprinkle with the parmesan and basil and slice to serve. **MAKES 4**

NOTE
+ This recipe begins with spelt dough – simply prepare the basic recipe until the end of step 3.

rustic olive, onion and rosemary flatbread

½ x quantity simple spelt loaf dough (see *basic recipe*)+
2 tablespoons rosemary leaves
1 brown onion, very thinly sliced
2 tablespoons extra virgin olive oil, plus extra for drizzling
½ teaspoon brown sugar
sea salt and cracked black pepper
½ cup (85g) green (Sicilian) olives, pitted and torn

Preheat oven to 200°C (400°F). Lightly grease a 20cm x 30cm slice tin. Press the dough into the tin and cover with plastic wrap. Set aside in a warm place for 1 hour or until doubled in size. Combine the rosemary, onion, oil, sugar, salt and pepper in a bowl. Gently press the olives into the dough. Spread with the onion mixture, drizzle with extra oil and bake for 20–25 minutes or until golden. **SERVES 6**

NOTE
+ This recipe begins with spelt dough – simply prepare the basic recipe until the end of step 3.

chapter two

NEED TO KNOW

salsa verde + fresh tomato salsa

buttermilk dressing + french vinaigrette + basil pesto + mayonnaise

salsa verde

2 cups flat-leaf parsley leaves
2 cups mint leaves
2 tablespoons baby capers, rinsed and drained
2 teaspoons Dijon mustard
1 teaspoon finely grated lemon rind
2 tablespoons lemon juice
½ cup (125ml) extra virgin olive oil
sea salt and cracked black pepper

Place the parsley, mint, capers, mustard, lemon rind, lemon juice, oil, salt and pepper in a small food processor. Process into a coarse paste. **MAKES 1 CUP**

TIPS
Fresh and zesty salsa verde, literally meaning 'green sauce', is a great all-rounder. Serve it with anything from roast lamb to grilled fish.
Parsley and mint make a good base for this sauce, but you can swap in other leafy herbs from your fridge or garden, too.

fresh tomato salsa

1 tomato, seeds removed and chopped into 1cm pieces
250g truss cherry tomatoes, quartered
¼ white onion, finely chopped
1 tablespoon chopped oregano leaves
2 tablespoons chopped basil leaves
2 tablespoons chopped mint leaves
1 tablespoon extra virgin olive oil
1 teaspoon red wine vinegar
sea salt and cracked black pepper

Place the tomato, cherry tomato, onion, oregano, basil and mint in a medium bowl. Add the oil, vinegar, salt and pepper and toss to combine. **MAKES 2¼ CUPS**

TIP
This summery salsa is perfect as part of a Mexican feast, or simply spoon it over barbecued meats or seafood.

buttermilk dressing

1 cup (250ml) buttermilk*
½ cup (140g) natural Greek-style (thick) yoghurt
1 teaspoon Dijon mustard
2 tablespoons white balsamic vinegar
1 teaspoon finely grated lemon rind
sea salt and cracked black pepper

Place the buttermilk, yoghurt, mustard, vinegar, lemon rind, salt and pepper in a medium bowl and whisk to combine. **MAKES 2 CUPS**

TIP
Creamy and a little tangy, this robust ranch-style dressing is perfect drizzled over crispy cos salads or crunchy slaws.

french vinaigrette

2 tablespoons red wine vinegar
¼ cup (60ml) extra virgin olive oil
1 teaspoon Dijon mustard
sea salt and cracked black pepper

Place the vinegar, oil, mustard, salt and pepper in a small bowl and whisk to combine. **MAKES ½ CUP**

TIP
Try making this vinaigrette in a small jar – seal and shake well to combine, then store any leftovers with ease.

basil pesto

2 cups basil leaves
½ clove garlic, crushed
¼ cup (40g) pine nuts, toasted
¼ cup (20g) finely grated parmesan
½ cup (125ml) extra virgin olive oil
sea salt and cracked black pepper

Place the basil, garlic, pine nuts, parmesan, oil, salt and pepper in a small food processor. Process into a coarse paste. **MAKES 1 CUP**

TIP
The fresh, full flavour of homemade pesto is hard to beat. Toss it through hot pasta, spread it over grilled meats or fish, or serve it as a dip with flatbreads.

mayonnaise

1 egg
1 tablespoon lemon juice
1 cup (250ml) light-flavoured extra virgin olive oil
sea salt flakes

Place the egg and lemon juice in a small food processor and process to combine. With the motor running, add the oil in a thin, steady stream. Add the salt and process for 30 seconds or until smooth and thickened. **MAKES 1¼ CUPS**

TIPS
You can try using macadamia oil (or any mild-flavoured nut oil) in place of the olive oil, if you prefer.
It's simple to add flavours to this mayonnaise – stir through lemon rind, chilli or roasted garlic.
Store mayonnaise in an airtight container or jar in the refrigerator for up to 1 week.

bechamel sauce + herb butter + caramelised onion

roasted garlic paste
+ classic gravy + quick hummus

bechamel sauce

40g unsalted butter, chopped
¼ cup (35g) plain (all-purpose) flour
2 cups (500ml) milk
sea salt and cracked black pepper

Melt the butter in a medium saucepan over
medium heat. Add the flour and cook, whisking,
for 1–2 minutes or until well combined and bubbling.
Gradually add the milk, whisking to combine, and
cook for 4–5 minutes or until thickened. Add salt
and pepper and whisk to combine. **MAKES 1 CUP**

TIP
*Master this classic white sauce for
use in gratins, lasagnes and as the
base for mac and cheese.*

herb butter

1 cup flat-leaf parsley leaves
¼ cup oregano leaves
¼ cup chopped chives
250g butter[+], softened

Place the parsley, oregano, chives and butter in
a small food processor. Process for 1–2 minutes
or until the herbs are finely chopped and the
mixture is well combined. **MAKES 1¼ CUPS**

NOTE
+ Choose a good-quality salted butter.
TIPS
*Melt this tasty butter over meats,
fish or vegetables, or simply
spread it onto warm toasted bread.*
**To make herb butter rounds, place
the mixture onto plastic wrap,
shape into a log, wrap and
refrigerate until firm. Slice to serve.**

caramelised onion

2 tablespoons extra virgin olive oil
4 brown onions (500g), thinly sliced
⅔ cup (150g) caster (superfine) sugar
1 teaspoon sea salt flakes
cracked black pepper
¼ cup (60ml) white wine vinegar

Heat the oil in a large non-stick frying pan over medium
heat. Add the onion and cook, stirring occasionally, for
12–14 minutes or until lightly browned. Add the sugar
and salt and cook for a further 6–8 minutes or until
caramelised. Add pepper and the vinegar and stir until
well combined. Allow to cool completely. **MAKES 1 CUP**

TIP
*Store caramelised onion in an
airtight container or jar in the
refrigerator for up to 2 weeks.*

roasted garlic paste

1 bulb garlic, halved horizontally
1 tablespoon extra virgin olive oil
sea salt flakes

Preheat oven to 180°C (350°F). Place the garlic, cut-side up, on a sheet of aluminium foil. Drizzle with the oil, sprinkle with salt and wrap to enclose. Place on an oven tray and roast for 30–40 minutes or until soft. Squeeze the garlic cloves from their skins into a bowl and mash with a fork until smooth. **MAKES ½ CUP**

TIPS
Once roasted, the garlic becomes soft, mellow and almost creamy, with a sweet caramelised flavour.
Brush it over the base of a pizza, knead it through dough or mix a little with butter and spread it onto warm crusty bread.

classic gravy

40g unsalted butter
2 tablespoons plain (all-purpose) flour
¼ cup (60ml) red wine
2 cups (500ml) beef or chicken stock
2 tablespoons pan drippings
cracked black pepper

Melt the butter in a small saucepan over medium heat. Add the flour and cook, whisking, for 1 minute or until well combined, golden brown and bubbling. Remove from the heat, add the wine and whisk to combine. Return to the heat and gradually add the stock and pan drippings, whisking to combine. Bring to a simmer and cook for 12–14 minutes or until thickened. Sprinkle with pepper to serve. **MAKES 1¼ CUPS**

quick hummus

1 x 400g can chickpeas (garbanzo beans),
    rinsed and drained
1 clove garlic
2 tablespoons lemon juice
¼ cup (60ml) water
⅓ cup (80ml) extra virgin olive oil
1 tablespoon tahini*
sea salt and cracked black pepper

Place the chickpeas, garlic, lemon juice, water, oil, tahini, salt and pepper in a small food processor. Process for 1–2 minutes or until smooth. **MAKES 1¼ CUPS**

TIPS
Making dips at home is satisfying and super easy – simply throw the ingredients for this hummus into a food processor and blitz.
Smooth, nutty hummus makes the perfect snack – try it with crudites or on flatbread with tabouli. It's also great as a side served with grilled meats.

couscous

1 cup (160g) whole-wheat couscous*
1 cup (250ml) boiling water or stock

Place the couscous in a large heatproof bowl. Add
the water, stir to combine and cover immediately
with plastic wrap or a tight-fitting lid. Allow to
stand for 5 minutes or until the water is absorbed.
Fluff the grains with a fork to serve. **MAKES 4 CUPS**

TIP
Serve couscous as a side to
braises and tagines, or use
it as a base for grain salads.

quinoa

1 cup (180g) quinoa
1¼ cups (310ml) water
sea salt flakes

Place the quinoa, water and salt in a medium
saucepan over high heat. Bring to the boil, reduce
the heat to low and cover with a tight-fitting lid.
Cook for 15 minutes or until just tender. Remove
from the heat and allow to steam for 10 minutes.
Fluff the seeds with a fork to serve. **MAKES 2¼ CUPS**

TIP
Use quinoa as you would rice.
It's great with stews, curries and
stir-fries, or as a base for salads.

white rice

1 cup (200g) white rice[+]
1½ cups (375ml) water
sea salt flakes

Place the rice, water and salt in a medium saucepan
over high heat and bring to the boil. Reduce the
heat to low, cover with a tight-fitting lid and cook
for 12 minutes or until just tender. Remove from
the heat and allow to steam for 8 minutes. Fluff the
grains with a fork to serve. **MAKES 2 CUPS**

NOTE
+ *This method will work well*
for most varieties of white rice,
including basmati and jasmine.

sushi rice

2½ cups (500g) sushi rice, rinsed and drained
3 cups (750ml) water
⅓ cup (80ml) rice wine vinegar
¼ cup (55g) caster (superfine) sugar
3 teaspoons sea salt flakes

Place the rice and water in a medium saucepan over
high heat and bring to the boil. Cook for 5 minutes.
Reduce the heat to low, cover with a tight-fitting lid
and cook for a further 10 minutes or until the rice is
just tender. Remove from the heat and allow to steam
for 5 minutes.

Place the vinegar, sugar and salt in a medium jug and
stir until the sugar and salt have dissolved. Add to the
rice and gently stir to combine. **MAKES 6 CUPS**

TIP
Use sushi rice for making nori rolls
or nigiri, or serve it in bowls as a
side to Asian-style fish or chicken.

couscous + quinoa + white rice + sushi rice

soft-boiled eggs + perfect poached eggs

soft-boiled eggs

1 litre water
1 teaspoon bicarbonate of (baking) soda
4 eggs, at room temperature
ice cubes and extra water, for cooling

Place the water and bicarbonate of soda in a small saucepan and bring to the boil over high heat. Gently lower the eggs into the saucepan[+] and cook for 5 minutes. Place ice cubes and extra water in a medium bowl. Using a slotted spoon, remove the eggs from the saucepan and place in the iced water to refresh. Carefully crack the shells and peel the eggs[++]. **MAKES 4**

NOTES
+ To prevent the eggs from cracking and hot water from splashing, carefully lower each egg into the boiling water using a spoon.
++ To serve the eggs in eggcups, simply crack and remove the tops of the shells and use teaspoons to eat.
TIPS
Cooking the eggs in water with bicarbonate of soda makes them easier to peel.
Transferring the eggs to iced water halts the cooking process, for perfectly runny, velvety yolks.

perfect poached eggs

2 tablespoons white vinegar
2 eggs, at room temperature

Half-fill a small saucepan with water and add the vinegar. Place over medium heat and bring to a rapid simmer. Break each egg into a small bowl. Reduce the heat to low and, using a spoon, gently swirl the water to create a whirlpool effect. Slide the eggs, one at a time, into the swirling water. Cook for 2–3 minutes or until the whites are opaque and the yolks are soft[+]. Using a slotted spoon, remove the eggs from the water. Drain well to serve. **MAKES 2**

NOTE
+ Press the eggs carefully with your fingertip to test how firm the yolks feel.
TIPS
The acid in the vinegar acts to keep the proteins in the eggwhites together.
Swirling the water also helps to keep the eggs in a neat oval shape.
Serve eggs on buttered sourdough toast sprinkled with cracked black pepper.
It's best to cook 2 eggs at a time. You can cook more, in batches of 2, in the same simmering water.

shortcrust pastry

2 cups (300g) plain (all-purpose) flour
175g cold unsalted butter, chopped
½ teaspoon sea salt flakes[+]
1 egg yolk
2 tablespoons iced water

Place the flour, butter and salt in a food processor and pulse until the mixture resembles fine breadcrumbs. With the motor running, add the egg yolk and water and process until a dough just comes together. Turn out onto a lightly floured surface, gently bring together to form a ball and flatten into a disc shape. Roll out between sheets of non-stick baking paper to 3mm thick and refrigerate for 1 hour. **MAKES 1 QUANTITY**

NOTE
+ To make sweet shortcrust pastry, replace the salt with ¼ cup (40g) sifted icing (confectioner's) sugar.

baked shortcrust pastry case

1 x quantity shortcrust pastry (see *basic recipe*, above)

Allow the pastry to stand at room temperature for 5 minutes or until workable. Use the pastry to line a lightly greased 22cm pie or tart tin. Trim the edges and prick the base with a fork. Refrigerate for 30 minutes.

Preheat oven to 180°C (350°F). Line the pastry case with non-stick baking paper and fill with baking weights or rice. Bake for 15 minutes, remove the paper and weights and bake for a further 15 minutes or until the pastry is golden and cooked through[+]. Allow to cool in the tin. **MAKES 1**

NOTE
+ If you're planning to bake the case again once it's filled, reduce the cooking time by 5 minutes, so the pastry is just set to the touch.

hot water pastry

150g unsalted butter, chopped
⅔ cup (160ml) water
2½ cups (375g) plain (all-purpose) flour
1 teaspoon sea salt flakes

Place the butter and water in a medium saucepan over high heat and bring to the boil. Remove from the heat and add the flour and salt. Mix to combine until a smooth dough forms. Turn out onto a lightly floured surface and knead until smooth and elastic. Roll out between sheets of non-stick baking paper to 5mm thick. **MAKES 1 QUANTITY**

TIP
Hot water pastry is simple to make and easy to handle. Use it to line anything from pies to fruit tarts.

shortcrust pastry + hot water pastry

cream cheese frosting + classic vanilla buttercream

candied citrus + mascarpone icing + pistachio praline

cream cheese frosting

250g cream cheese, softened
¼ cup (60g) fresh ricotta
½ cup (80g) icing (confectioner's) sugar, sifted
1 tablespoon lemon juice

Place the cream cheese, ricotta, sugar and lemon juice in the bowl of an electric mixer and whisk on medium speed for 5 minutes or until smooth. **MAKES 1¼ CUPS**

TIPS
Spread this luscious tangy frosting over carrot cake, red velvet cupcakes or a banana loaf cake.
To make vanilla cream cheese frosting, simply swap the lemon juice for 1 teaspoon vanilla extract.

classic vanilla buttercream

250g unsalted butter, softened
1 cup (160g) icing (confectioner's) sugar, sifted
1 teaspoon vanilla extract

Place the butter and sugar in the bowl of an electric mixer and beat on medium speed, scraping down the sides of the bowl, for 6–8 minutes or until pale and creamy. Add the vanilla and beat for a further 2 minutes or until well combined. **MAKES 1¼ CUPS**

TIPS
Delightfully smooth and sweet, buttercream is perfect for piping or spreading onto cute cupcakes and clever birthday cakes.
You can stir through 1 or 2 drops of food colouring, if you wish.

candied citrus

1 cup (250ml) water
1 cup (220g) caster (superfine) sugar
400g citrus fruit (about 2 pieces)[+], trimmed
    and thinly sliced

Place the water and sugar in a small saucepan over low heat and stir until the sugar has dissolved. Increase the heat to medium, add the fruit and bring to a simmer. Reduce the heat to low and cook for 1 hour or until the pith is translucent. Transfer the fruit to a wire rack set over a tray lined with non-stick baking paper to cool, allowing the excess syrup to drain. **MAKES 1 QUANTITY**

NOTE
+ You can candy your choice of citrus fruit – oranges, blood oranges, lemons and grapefruits all work well.
TIP
Use jewel-like candied citrus to adorn cakes, slices, homemade chocolates and desserts.

mascarpone icing

1 cup (250ml) single (pouring) cream*
1 cup (250g) mascarpone*
½ cup (80g) icing (confectioner's) sugar, sifted

Place the cream, mascarpone and sugar
in the bowl of an electric mixer and whisk
until soft peaks form. **MAKES 2 CUPS**

___

TIP
*This smooth, pillowy icing is similar
to whipped cream but with more flavour
and a little extra hold. It's perfect piled
onto almost any cake or cupcake, and
makes a lovely filling for a sponge.*

pistachio praline

2 cups (440g) white (granulated) sugar
¼ cup (60ml) water
½ cup (70g) shelled pistachios

Place the sugar and water in a large saucepan over
high heat and cook, stirring until the sugar dissolves,
for 8–10 minutes or until dark golden[+]. Pour onto a
lightly greased baking tray lined with non-stick baking
paper, tilting to create a thin, even layer. Sprinkle
with the pistachios and allow to cool completely on the
tray. Roughly chop the praline to serve. **MAKES 1 QUANTITY**

___

NOTE
*+ Take extra care to ensure the sugar
mixture doesn't burn.*
TIPS
*You can swap pistachios for your
favourite nuts. Almonds and hazelnuts
both work well.*
**Keep praline on-hand for sprinkling
over ice-cream or desserts. Store in an
airtight container for up to 2 weeks.**

chapter three
_____

SWEET

DARK CHOCOLATE GANACHE

DARK CHOCOLATE GANACHE

1¾ cups (430ml) single (pouring) cream*

600g dark (55%) chocolate, grated or finely chopped[+]

STEP 1 Place the cream in a small saucepan over medium heat. Cook, stirring occasionally, until hot but not boiling[++].

STEP 2 Place the chocolate in a large bowl and add the cream, stirring once to remove any chocolate from the base of the bowl. Allow to stand for 2 minutes.

STEP 3 Stir the ganache gently until just combined. **MAKES 2¾ CUPS**

NOTES

+ You can place roughly broken chocolate in a food processor to finely chop, if you prefer.
++ If you have a sugar thermometer, use it to help you measure the temperature of the cream. Remove the cream from the heat at 85–95°C (185–200°F). It will look as though it's just beginning to bubble from below. If you accidentally boil the cream, it's best to start again as this can split the ganache.

dark chocolate and raspberry tart

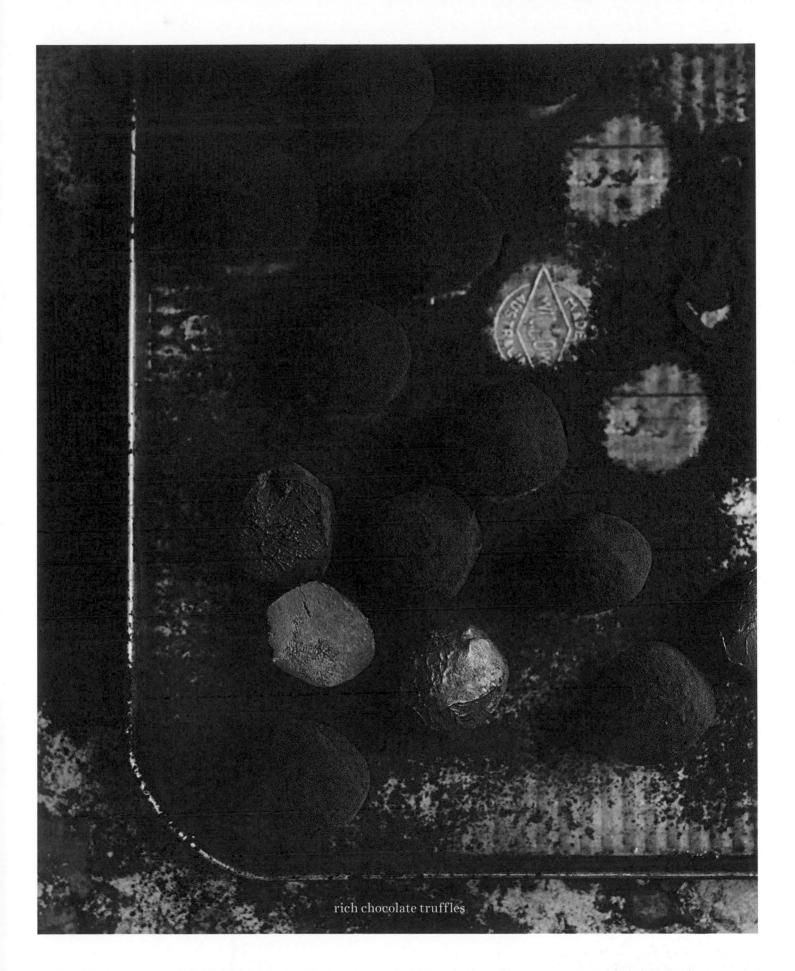

rich chocolate truffles

dark chocolate and raspberry tart

1 x quantity dark chocolate ganache (see *basic recipe*),
   still warm
250g raspberries
chocolate pastry
¼ cup (25g) Dutch cocoa*
1½ cups (225g) plain (all-purpose) flour
125g cold unsalted butter, chopped
½ cup (80g) icing (confectioner's) sugar
3 egg yolks
1 tablespoon iced water

To make the chocolate pastry, place the cocoa, flour, butter and sugar in a food processor and process until the mixture resembles fine breadcrumbs. With the motor running, add the egg yolks and water and process until a dough just comes together. Turn out onto a lightly floured surface and gently bring together until smooth. Roll out between sheets of non-stick baking paper to 4mm thick. Refrigerate for 1 hour.

Use the pastry to line a lightly greased 26cm round loose-bottomed fluted tart tin[+]. Trim the edges and prick the base with a fork. Refrigerate for 30 minutes.

Preheat oven to 180°C (350°F). Line the pastry case with non-stick baking paper, fill with baking weights or rice and bake for 15 minutes. Remove the paper and weights and bake for a further 10 minutes or until the pastry is just cooked. Allow to cool in the tin.

Pour the ganache into the tart case and refrigerate for 1 hour or until set. Remove the tart from the tin, place on a serving plate and top with the raspberries. Slice to serve. **SERVES 6–8**

NOTE
+ If the pastry is too firm to handle straight from the fridge, allow it to warm to room temperature for a few minutes.

rich chocolate truffles

1 x quantity dark chocolate ganache (see *basic recipe*), cooled
Dutch cocoa*, for dusting

Refrigerate the ganache for 3 hours or until completely set.

Roll heaped teaspoons of the ganache into balls and place on a tray[+]. Dust with cocoa to coat[++]. Store truffles in the refrigerator and remove 5 minutes before serving. **MAKES 45**

NOTES
+ It helps to regularly wash your hands in cold water when rolling the truffles.
*++ **Keep truffles refrigerated, between sheets of non-stick baking paper, in an airtight container for up to 1 week.***

whipped chocolate ganache

1 x quantity dark chocolate ganache (see *basic recipe*),
   still warm

Place the ganache over a bowl of iced water. Whisk gently for 3–5 minutes or until slightly thickened[+]. Use whipped ganache immediately[++]. **MAKES 2¾ CUPS**

NOTES
+ The ganache will set a little further after whisking, so don't be tempted to overwhip it. If the whipped ganache does become too firm, the easiest way to soften it again is to place it in a heatproof bowl over a saucepan of simmering water. Stir until it's more workable.
*++ **Use this rich, fluffy ganache as you would icing – layer it between cakes, pipe it onto cupcakes or spread it over cookies to make cookie sandwiches.***

whipped chocolate ganache

the basic

NO-FAIL MERINGUE MIXTURE

the perfect pavlova

NO-FAIL MERINGUE MIXTURE

225ml eggwhite (about 6 eggs)[+]

1½ cups (330g) caster (superfine) sugar

1 tablespoon cornflour (cornstarch)

1½ teaspoons white vinegar

STEP 1 Place the eggwhite in the bowl of an electric mixer and whisk on high speed until soft peaks form.

STEP 2 Add the sugar, 1 tablespoon at a time, whisking until each addition is dissolved before adding more[++].

STEP 3 Once all the sugar has been added, scrape down the sides of the bowl and whisk for a further 10–15 minutes or until the mixture is thick and glossy[+++].

STEP 4 Place the cornflour and vinegar in a small bowl and mix until smooth.

STEP 5 Add the cornflour mixture to the eggwhite mixture and whisk for 30 seconds or until well combined[++++]. **MAKES 1 QUANTITY**

NOTES

+ *Making meringue is a science. Be sure to measure your ingredients carefully, including the eggwhites as egg sizes do vary. Fresh, room temperature eggs work best – when whisked they'll become fluffy and voluminous, plus they're more stable during baking.*

++ ***Be patient when gradually adding the sugar to the eggwhite. Each tablespoon of sugar should be dissolved before the next is added.***

+++ *Take care not to overwhisk the meringue mixture – it's ready when it's thick, glossy, smooth and there are no more sugar granules. You can check this by rubbing a little mixture between your thumb and forefinger.*

++++ ***See the recipes that follow for how to bake this meringue mixture.***

TIP

It's best to avoid making meringue on humid days. Excess humidity can cause meringue to sink during or after baking.

salted caramel meringues + chocolate meringues + rosewater and pistachio meringues + raspberry meringues

the perfect pavlova

1 x quantity no-fail meringue mixture (see *basic recipe*)
1½ cups (375ml) single (pouring) cream*, whipped
raspberries, passionfruit pulp and sliced peaches, to serve

Preheat oven to 150°C (300°F). Using a pencil, draw a 20cm circle on a sheet of non-stick baking paper. Place the baking paper, pencil-side down, on a lightly greased baking tray+. Spoon the meringue mixture into the circle to make a neat round. Reduce the oven temperature to 120°C (250°F) and bake for 1 hour. Allow to cool completely in the closed oven++.

Place the pavlova on a cake stand or plate and top with the whipped cream, raspberries, passionfruit and peach to serve. **SERVES 8–10**

NOTES
+ Turn the baking paper so it's pencil-side down on the tray – no marks will transfer onto the meringue.
*++ **Allow the meringue to cool gradually in the oven with the door closed – preferably overnight.***

salted caramel meringues

1 x quantity no-fail meringue mixture (see *basic recipe*)
2 tablespoons creamy caramel (see *basic recipe*, page 264)
   or store-bought caramel
sea salt flakes, for sprinkling

Preheat oven to 150°C (300°F). Spoon 6 x 10cm rounds of the meringue mixture onto a baking tray lined with non-stick baking paper. Swirl a little of the caramel through each round and top with salt. Reduce the oven temperature to 120°C (250°F) and bake for 40 minutes. Allow to cool in the closed oven. **MAKES 6**

chocolate meringues

1 x quantity no-fail meringue mixture (see *basic recipe*)
50g dark chocolate, melted and cooled to room temperature

Preheat oven to 150°C (300°F). Spoon 6 x 10cm rounds of the meringue mixture onto a baking tray lined with non-stick baking paper. Swirl a little of the chocolate through each round. Reduce the oven temperature to 120°C (250°F) and bake for 40 minutes. Allow to cool completely in the closed oven. **MAKES 6**

rosewater and pistachio meringues

¼ teaspoon rosewater*
1 x quantity no-fail meringue mixture (see *basic recipe*)
½ cup (65g) slivered or chopped pistachios

Preheat oven to 150°C (300°F). Add the rosewater to the meringue mixture and whisk to combine. Spoon 6 x 10cm rounds onto a baking tray lined with non-stick baking paper and top with the pistachio. Reduce the oven temperature to 120°C (250°F) and bake for 40 minutes. Allow to cool completely in the closed oven. **MAKES 6**

raspberry meringues

1 cup (130g) frozen raspberries, thawed and processed
   into puree
½ cup (110g) caster (superfine) sugar
1 x quantity no-fail meringue mixture (see *basic recipe*)

Preheat oven to 150°C (300°F). Strain the raspberry into a small saucepan. Place over medium heat, add the sugar and stir until dissolved. Simmer for 5 minutes. Allow to cool. Spoon 6 x 10cm rounds of the meringue mixture onto a baking tray lined with non-stick baking paper. Swirl a little of the raspberry through each round. Reduce the oven temperature to 120°C (250°F) and bake for 40 minutes. Allow to cool completely in the closed oven. **MAKES 6**

lemon meringue pie

1 x quantity sweet baked shortcrust pastry case
   (see *basic recipe*, page 220), still in tin and cooled
1 x quantity classic lemon curd (see *basic recipe*, page 286)
   or 1½ cups (480g) store-bought lemon curd
1 x quantity no-fail meringue mixture (see *basic recipe*)

Preheat oven grill (broiler) to high. Place the pastry case on an oven tray. Pour the lemon curd into the pastry case and smooth the top, using a palette knife. Spoon the meringue mixture over the lemon curd and grill for 2–3 minutes or until the peaks of the meringue are golden brown. Alternatively use a small hand-held kitchen blowtorch to brown the meringue. Allow to cool, place the pie on a cake stand or plate and slice to serve. **SERVES 8**

lemon meringue pie

the basic

CHEWY CHOCOLATE CHIP COOKIES

CHEWY CHOCOLATE CHIP COOKIES

200g cold unsalted butter, chopped

1 cup (175g) brown sugar

¾ cup (165g) white (granulated) sugar

1 teaspoon vanilla extract

2 tablespoons milk

1 egg

2 cups (300g) plain (all-purpose) flour

¼ teaspoon baking powder

¼ teaspoon bicarbonate of (baking) soda

¼ teaspoon table salt

300g dark chocolate, chopped

STEP 1 Preheat oven to 180°C (350°F).

STEP 2 Place the butter and both the sugars in the bowl of an electric mixer and beat on low speed until just combined.

STEP 3 Increase the speed to medium and beat for 8 minutes or until pale and creamy, scraping down the sides of the bowl.

STEP 4 Add the vanilla, milk and egg and beat for 2 minutes or until light and fluffy.

STEP 5 Sift in the flour, baking powder, bicarbonate of soda and salt and beat until combined.

STEP 6 Add the chocolate and stir to combine.

STEP 7 Roll heaped tablespoons of the mixture into balls and place on lightly greased baking trays lined with non-stick baking paper[+]. Bake for 12–14 minutes or until golden brown[++].

STEP 8 Allow to cool on the trays for 5 minutes before transferring onto wire racks to cool. **MAKES 22**

NOTES
+ Leave 2–3cm between each ball of cookie dough to allow for spreading in the oven.
*++ **Cookies should be golden around the edges with even colouring on the base when they're ready.***
TIP
If you're baking more than one tray of cookies at a time, swap their shelf positions in the oven halfway through cooking time to ensure even colouring.

whipped peanut butter cookie sandwiches

s'mores

cookies and cream ice-cream + cookies and cream popsicles (*opposite*)

whipped peanut butter cookie sandwiches

1 cup (160g) icing (confectioner's) sugar mixture
1 cup (280g) smooth peanut butter
80g unsalted butter, softened
1 teaspoon vanilla extract
⅓ cup (80ml) single (pouring) cream*
1 x batch chewy chocolate chip cookies (see *basic recipe*)

Place the icing sugar mixture, peanut butter, butter and vanilla in the bowl of an electric mixer. Beat on medium speed for 4 minutes or until well combined. Add the cream and beat for a further 1 minute or until light and fluffy.

Spread the bases of 11 of the cookies with the peanut butter mixture and sandwich with the remaining cookies. **MAKES 11**

s'mores

1 x batch chewy chocolate chip cookies (see *basic recipe*)
11 squares dark chocolate
11 white marshmallows

Preheat oven to 180°C (350°F). Arrange the cookies, base-side up, on lightly greased baking trays lined with non-stick baking paper. Place 1 square of chocolate on each of half the cookies. Place the marshmallows on the remaining cookies. Bake for 1–2 minutes or until the chocolate is melted and the marshmallows have softened. Sandwich the marshmallow cookies with the chocolate cookies to serve. **MAKES 11**

cookies and cream ice-cream

2 litres vanilla ice-cream, chopped
½ x batch chewy chocolate chip cookies (see *basic recipe*), finely chopped

Place the ice-cream in the bowl of an electric mixer and beat on low speed for 2 minutes or until soft. Add half the cookie crumbs and beat until just combined.

Spoon the mixture into a 2-litre-capacity metal container⁺, cover with plastic wrap and freeze for 3 hours or overnight until solid. Sprinkle with the remaining cookie to serve. **SERVES 8**

NOTE
+ *To make cookies and cream popsicles, simply divide the unfrozen ice-cream mixture between 12 x ⅓-cup-capacity (80ml) popsicle moulds and insert popsicle sticks. Freeze for 3 hours or until solid. Press the popsicles into the remaining cookie crumbs to serve.*

CARAMELISED SUMMER FRUIT

CARAMELISED SUMMER FRUIT

½ cup (125ml) apple juice or water

½ cup (110g) caster (superfine) sugar

2 vanilla beans, split and seeds scraped

6 apricots (500g), halved and stones removed

6 plums (600g), halved and stones removed

4 yellow peaches (500g), halved and stones removed

STEP 1 Preheat oven grill (broiler) to medium.

STEP 2 Pour the apple juice into a large lightly greased oven tray lined with non-stick baking paper.

STEP 3 Place the sugar and vanilla seeds in a medium bowl and rub well to combine, using your fingertips.

STEP 4 Press the cut sides of the fruit into the vanilla sugar and place, cut-side up, on the tray.

STEP 5 Sprinkle the fruit with any remaining vanilla sugar and top with the vanilla pods.

STEP 6 Grill for 10–15 minutes or until the fruit is caramelised but not collapsed. Allow to cool slightly. Remove and discard the vanilla pods before serving. **SERVES 8**

TIPS

A clever solution to an overflowing summer fruit bowl, you can mix and match your favourite stone fruits for this recipe. All varieties of cherries, nectarines, plums and peaches work well.
Store caramelised fruit in the refrigerator for up to 1 week.

caramelised summer fruit with torched meringue

granola cups with caramelised summer fruit

caramelised summer fruit with torched meringue

1 x quantity caramelised summer fruit (see *basic recipe*),
  heated through
1 x no-fail meringue mixture
  (see *basic recipe*, page 240)

Preheat oven grill (broiler) to high. Place the fruit and
any syrup in a 15cm x 25cm ovenproof dish. Spoon the
meringue over the fruit. Grill for 2–3 minutes or until the
meringue is just cooked and the peaks are golden brown[+].
Spoon onto serving plates and serve immediately. **SERVES 8**

NOTE
*+ You can also use a small hand-held
kitchen blowtorch to brown the meringue.*

granola cups with caramelised summer fruit

1 x quantity caramelised summer fruit (see *basic recipe*)
3 cups (840g) natural Greek-style (thick) yoghurt
3 cups (390g) store-bought granola

Divide the fruit and any syrup between serving cups or
bowls. Top with the yoghurt and granola to serve. **MAKES 6**

TIP
*To make granola and caramelised fruit
parfaits, simply layer the fruit, yoghurt
and granola in serving glasses or jars.*

caramelised summer fruit frozen yoghurt

1kg natural Greek-style (thick) yoghurt
¾ cup (270g) honey
1 teaspoon vanilla extract
½ x quantity caramelised summer fruit (see *basic recipe*),
  cooled and chopped

Place the yoghurt, honey and vanilla in a medium bowl
and mix to combine. Transfer to a large zip-lock plastic
bag and press any air out. Seal and freeze for 3–4 hours
or until solid.

Break the frozen yoghurt up and place in a food
processor[+]. Process until smooth, scraping down the
sides of the bowl. Pour into a 2-litre-capacity metal
container. Spoon the fruit over the yoghurt mixture
and, using a spoon, swirl to combine. Freeze for
3–4 hours or overnight until solid.

Allow the frozen yoghurt to stand at room temperature
for 5 minutes before scooping into serving bowls to serve.
SERVES 8

NOTE
*+ To break the frozen yoghurt into
pieces, you can bend it and tap it
on your benchtop while it's still in
the zip-lock bag. Then simply unseal
and empty into the food processor.*

caramelised summer fruit frozen yoghurt

the basic

CREAMY CARAMEL

CREAMY CARAMEL

1½ cups (375ml) single (pouring) cream*

180g unsalted butter

3 cups (660g) caster (superfine) sugar

1 cup (250ml) water

STEP 1 Place the cream and butter in a small saucepan over medium heat and bring to the boil. Remove from the heat and set aside.

STEP 2 Place the sugar and water in a medium saucepan over high heat and cook, stirring with a metal spoon until combined. Bring to the boil and cook without stirring, until the temperature reaches 180°C (350°F) on a sugar thermometer and the mixture is golden in colour[+].

STEP 3 Remove from the heat and, working quickly, add the butter mixture in a thin steady stream, stirring to combine.

STEP 4 Return the pan to low heat and cook, stirring, for 5 minutes or until the caramel has thickened slightly.

STEP 5 Pour into a bowl and allow to cool to room temperature. **MAKES 3½ CUPS**

NOTE

+ For a richer caramel with a subtle burnt flavour, let the sugar and water cook until it's a little deeper in colour, or 185°C (365°F).

TIPS

It's worth investing in a sugar (or candy) thermometer. They're available at kitchen shops and some supermarkets, and take the guesswork out of heating creams and sugar syrups for homemade treats. **Store creamy caramel, in an airtight container or jar, in the refrigerator for up to 1 week.**

To make salted caramel, simply stir in 1 teaspoon of sea salt flakes at step 4.

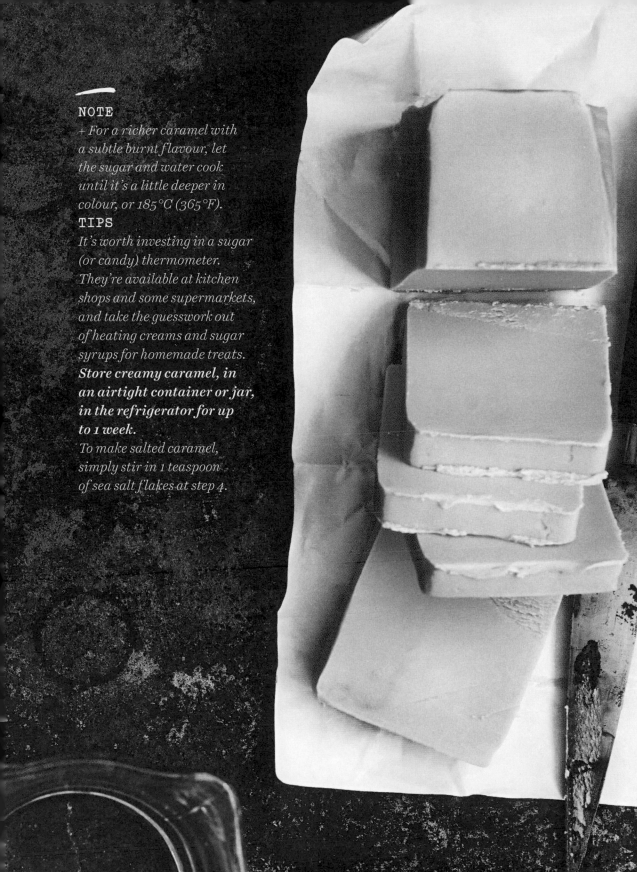

salted chocolate caramel tarts

apple tarte tatin

salted caramel ice-cream sundaes

salted chocolate caramel tarts

250g store-bought ginger nut biscuits*
100g unsalted butter, melted
½ x quantity creamy caramel (see *basic recipe*), cooled
80g dark chocolate, melted
sea salt flakes, for sprinkling

Place the biscuits in a food processor and process until finely chopped. Add the butter and process until well combined. Press the mixture into the base and sides of 4 x 11cm round loose-bottomed fluted tart tins and refrigerate for 20 minutes or until firm.

Divide the caramel between the tart bases and refrigerate for 10 minutes or until set.

Spoon the chocolate onto the tarts and allow to set. Remove from the tins and sprinkle with salt to serve. **MAKES 4**

apple tarte tatin

1 sheet (375g) store-bought butter puff pastry*, thawed
½ cup (160g) creamy caramel (see *basic recipe*),
  plus extra to serve
3 Granny Smith (green) apples (540g), peeled,
  quartered, cored and cut into 1cm wedges
vanilla ice-cream, to serve

Preheat oven to 220°C (425°F). Using a small sharp knife, trim the pastry into a 30cm round and make a small cross incision in the centre. Refrigerate until ready to use.

Place the caramel in a 26cm round ovenproof non-stick frying pan over medium heat and bring to the boil. Add the apple and cook for 5–6 minutes or until just softened. Remove from the heat and top with the pastry round. Place the pan on an oven tray. Bake for 15 minutes or until the pastry is golden and puffed. Allow to cool slightly.

Invert onto a lightly greased baking tray lined with non-stick baking paper. Bake for a further 5 minutes or until the apples are golden and caramelised. Serve warm with ice-cream and extra caramel. **SERVES 4-6**

salted caramel ice-cream sundaes

4 litres vanilla ice-cream, chopped
½ x quantity creamy caramel (see *basic recipe*), cooled
1 cup (100g) shaved white chocolate
1 tablespoon black sea salt flakes or regular sea salt flakes+

Place the ice-cream in the bowl of an electric mixer and beat for 2 minutes or until soft. Transfer to a 2-litre-capacity metal container. Add 1 cup (320g) of the caramel and swirl through, using a butter knife. Freeze overnight or until firm.

Place scoops of the ice-cream into serving bowls and top with the remaining caramel. Sprinkle with the chocolate and salt to serve. **MAKES 8**

NOTE
+ *You can buy black sea salt flakes at specialty food shops and some supermarkets. Substitute with regular sea salt flakes, if you prefer.*

the basic

GRANITA SUGAR SYRUP

watermelon and mint granita

GRANITA SUGAR SYRUP

1 cup (220g) caster (superfine) sugar

1½ cups (375ml) water

STEP 1 Place the sugar and water in a small saucepan over low heat. Cook, stirring, until the sugar has dissolved. Allow to cool slightly[+]. **MAKES 1 QUANTITY**

—

NOTE
+ *See the recipes that follow for how to use this syrup to make icy treats.*

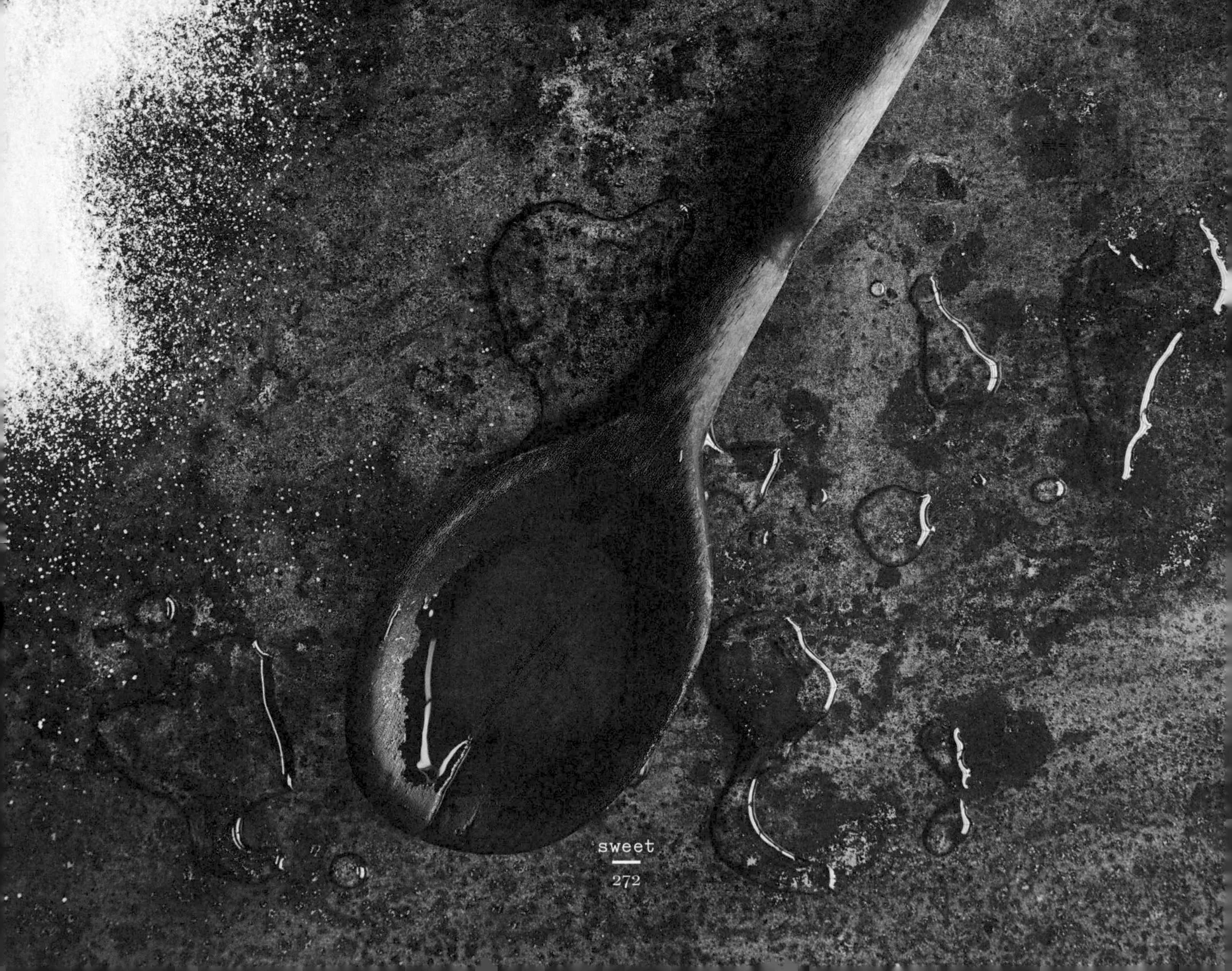

icy lattes

watermelon and mint granita

3 cups (500g) chopped watermelon[+]
1 cup baby (micro) mint or ¼ cup finely chopped mint leaves
2 tablespoons lemon juice
1 x quantity granita sugar syrup (see *basic recipe*)

Place the watermelon in a blender and blend until smooth. Strain into a large jug, discarding any solids. Add the mint, lemon juice and granita syrup and stir until well combined. Pour into a shallow metal container and allow to cool. Freeze for 4 hours or until firm.

Using a fork, scrape the granita into icy crystals. Spoon into serving glasses to serve. **SERVES 6**

NOTE
+ You'll need to buy about 1kg watermelon to get the 500g peeled flesh needed for this recipe.

icy lattes

4 x 30ml shots espresso[+]
1½ cups (375ml) milk
1 x quantity granita sugar syrup (see *basic recipe*)
½ cup (125ml) single (pouring) cream*

Place the espresso, milk and granita syrup in a large jug and stir until well combined. Pour into a shallow metal container and allow to cool. Freeze for 4 hours or until firm.

Place the cream in the bowl of an electric mixer and whisk until soft peaks form. Using a fork, scrape the granita into icy crystals. Spoon into serving glasses and top with the cream to serve. **SERVES 6**

NOTE
+ If you don't have access to an espresso machine, you can use ½ cup (125ml) of strong brewed or percolated coffee instead.

lychee lime snow

1 x 500g can pitted lychees, drained
2 tablespoons lime juice
1 x quantity granita sugar syrup (see *basic recipe*)
finely grated lime rind, to serve

Place the lychees in a blender and blend until smooth. Add the lime juice and granita syrup and blend until well combined. Pour into a shallow metal container and allow to cool. Freeze for 4 hours or until firm.

Using a fork, scrape the granita into icy crystals. Spoon into serving cups and top with lime rind to serve. **SERVES 6**

TIP
These summertime cups are just as good for a fun afternoon snack as they are for an elegant, refreshing dessert.

lychee lime snow

the basic

CHOCOLATE FUDGE CAKE

CHOCOLATE FUDGE CAKE

250g unsalted butter, chopped

300g dark (70%) chocolate, chopped

2 tablespoons Dutch cocoa*, sifted

½ cup (125ml) milk

6 eggs

1 cup (220g) caster (superfine) sugar

½ cup (85g) brown sugar

1 cup (150g) plain (all-purpose) flour

STEP 1 Place the butter and chocolate in a medium saucepan over low heat and stir until melted and smooth. Add the cocoa and milk and stir to combine. Set aside to cool slightly.

STEP 2 Place the eggs and both the sugars in the bowl of an electric mixer and whisk on high speed for 12–15 minutes or until pale, thick and creamy.

STEP 3 Add the chocolate mixture to the egg mixture and whisk, scraping down the sides of the bowl, until just combined. Reduce the speed to low, add the flour and whisk until just combined.

STEP 4 Preheat oven to 160°C (325°F).

STEP 5 Lightly grease a 22cm round springform cake tin and line with non-stick baking paper.

STEP 6 Pour the cake mixture into the tin and bake for 1 hour – 1 hour 10 minutes or until set[+]. Allow to cool completely in the tin.

STEP 7 Remove the cake from the tin to serve. **SERVES 8–10**

NOTE
+ The cake is ready when it feels set to the touch. If tested, a wooden skewer will not come out clean – the cake will set with a fudgy centre as it cools.

molten chocolate puddings

chocolate fudge cupcakes

molten chocolate puddings

1 x quantity chocolate fudge cake mixture (see *basic recipe*)[+]
Dutch cocoa*, for dusting

Preheat oven to 200°C (400°F). Heat a baking tray in the oven for 5 minutes. Lightly grease 12 x ¾-cup-capacity (180ml) metal pudding moulds or ovenproof ramekins. Pour ½ cup (125ml) of the cake mixture into each mould. Transfer to the hot baking tray and bake for 12 minutes or until just set to the touch. Allow to cool in the moulds for 1 minute before turning out onto serving plates. Dust with cocoa and serve immediately. **MAKES 12**

NOTE
+ This recipe begins with uncooked cake mixture – simply prepare the basic recipe until the end of step 3.
TIP
These melt-in-your-mouth puddings are best served warm, either dusted in cocoa or topped with berries and double cream.

chocolate fudge cupcakes

1 x quantity chocolate fudge cake mixture (see *basic recipe*)[+]
½ x quantity whipped chocolate ganache
   (see *recipe*, page 236)

Preheat oven to 160°C (325°F). Line 18 x ½-cup-capacity (125ml) muffin tins with paper cases. Divide the cake mixture between the tins and bake for 20–22 minutes or until set to the touch. Allow to cool in the tins completely.
   Remove the cupcakes from the tins and spread with the whipped ganache to serve. **MAKES 18**

NOTE
+ This recipe begins with uncooked cake mixture – simply prepare the basic recipe until the end of step 3.

chocolate fudge and salted caramel layer cake

1 x quantity chocolate fudge cake mixture (see *basic recipe*)[+]
1 x quantity whipped chocolate ganache
   (see *recipe*, page 236)
⅓ cup (100g) creamy caramel (see *basic recipe*, page 264) or
   store-bought caramel
black sea salt flakes or regular sea salt flakes[++], for sprinkling

Preheat oven to 160°C (325°F). Lightly grease 2 x 20cm round springform cake tins and line with non-stick baking paper. Divide the cake mixture evenly between the tins and bake for 30–35 minutes or until set to the touch. Allow to cool completely in the tins. Refrigerate for 1 hour or until chilled.
   Remove the cakes from the tins and, using a serrated knife, cut each cake in half horizontally.
   To assemble, place a base layer of cake, cut-side up, on a cake stand or plate. Spread with ½ cup (125ml) of the ganache and drizzle with 2 tablespoons of the caramel. Repeat twice more and top with the final layer of cake, cut-side down. Spread the remaining ganache onto the cake and sprinkle with salt to serve. **SERVES 12**

NOTES
+ This recipe begins with uncooked cake mixture – simply prepare the basic recipe until the end of step 3.
++ You can buy black sea salt flakes at specialty food shops and some supermarkets. Substitute with regular sea salt flakes, if you prefer.
TIP
It's a good idea to use the measurements given when spreading the ganache and drizzling the caramel. It makes for a more stable finish and nice even layers, which look great when the cake is sliced.

chocolate fudge and salted caramel layer cake

the basic

CLASSIC LEMON CURD

CLASSIC LEMON CURD

2 eggs

2 egg yolks, extra

1 cup (220g) caster (superfine) sugar

1 tablespoon finely grated lemon rind

½ cup (125ml) lemon juice

150g cold unsalted butter, chopped into 2cm cubes

STEP 1 Place the eggs, extra yolks, sugar, lemon rind and lemon juice in a medium bowl and whisk to combine.

STEP 2 Transfer the mixture to a large saucepan over medium heat and cook, stirring, for 2 minutes or until the sugar has dissolved.

STEP 3 Reduce the heat to low and add the butter, 3 pieces at a time, stirring continuously until melted.

STEP 4 Cook, stirring constantly, for a further 4–6 minutes or until the curd has thickened and coats the back of a spoon.

STEP 5 Immediately strain into a heatproof bowl, discarding any solids. Allow to cool slightly and cover with plastic wrap. Refrigerate for 1 hour or until chilled. **MAKES 1½ CUPS**

TIPS
By constantly stirring the mixture, you'll end up with luscious, velvety smooth curd.
Store lemon curd in an airtight container or jar in the refrigerator for up to 1 week.

lemon and blueberry layer cake

cheat's lemon meringue parfaits

lemon and blueberry layer cake

1 x quantity my nan's sponge cake (see *basic recipe*, page 318)
    or 2 store-bought 20cm round sponge cakes
2 cups (500ml) single (pouring) cream*
1 cup (250g) mascarpone*
1 teaspoon vanilla extract
¼ cup (40g) icing (confectioner's) sugar, sifted
½ x quantity classic lemon curd (see *basic recipe*)
250g blueberries

Using a serrated knife, cut the cakes in half horizontally.
    Place the cream, mascarpone, vanilla and sugar in the bowl of an electric mixer and whisk until soft peaks form.
    To assemble the cake, place a base layer of sponge, cut-side up, on a cake stand or plate. Spread with 1 cup (250ml) of the mascarpone cream and drizzle with 2 tablespoons of the lemon curd. Repeat twice more and top with the final layer of sponge. Spoon the remaining mascarpone cream onto the cake and swirl through the remaining curd. Sprinkle with the blueberries to serve. **SERVES 8–10**

TIPS
Blueberries, lemon and mascarpone are a match made in heaven, but you can top this cake with any berries you like, or even fresh passionfruit pulp.
It's a good idea to use the measurements given when spreading the mascarpone cream and drizzling the lemon curd. It makes for even layers and a stable cake.

Cheat's lemon meringue parfaits

1 cup (250ml) single (pouring) cream*
1 teaspoon vanilla bean paste
1 x quantity classic lemon curd (see *basic recipe*)
100g store-bought meringues, crushed

Place the cream and vanilla in the bowl of an electric mixer and whisk until soft peaks form. Add half the lemon curd and fold to combine.
    Divide the remaining lemon curd between serving glasses and top with the lemon cream. Sprinkle with the meringue to serve. **MAKES 6**

TIP
Tart, sunny lemon curd shines in these simple desserts, with meringue on top for a sweet crunch. A cinch to prepare when entertaining, serve them in rustic jars, glasses or small bowls.

vanilla and lemon swirl ice-cream

2 litres vanilla ice-cream, chopped
1 x quantity classic lemon curd (see *basic recipe*)

Place the ice-cream in the bowl of an electric mixer and beat for 2 minutes or until softened. Spread into a 2-litre-capacity metal container, spoon over the lemon curd and swirl through using a butter knife. Freeze for 3 hours or overnight until solid.
    Scoop into serving bowls to serve. **SERVES 8**

TIPS
Swirl the curd gently through the ice-cream to create beautiful folds of lemon yellow.
Serve scoops of the ice-cream in waffle cones for an easy after-dinner treat or summery snack.

vanilla and lemon swirl ice-cream

the basic

MOLTEN CHOC-CHUNK BROWNIES

MOLTEN CHOC-CHUNK BROWNIES

1 cup (150g) plain (all-purpose) flour

¾ cup (75g) cocoa

¾ cup (130g) brown sugar

1⅓ cups (290g) caster (superfine) sugar

175g unsalted butter, melted and cooled

1 teaspoon vanilla extract

3 eggs

125g dark chocolate, chopped

STEP 1 Place the flour, cocoa, both the sugars, the butter, vanilla and eggs in a large bowl and mix until smooth.

STEP 2 Add the chocolate and stir to combine.

STEP 3 Preheat oven to 160°C (325°F).

STEP 4 Lightly grease a 20cm square tin and line with non-stick baking paper.

STEP 5 Spread the mixture into the tin.

STEP 6 Bake for 50 minutes – 1 hour or until the brownie is set[+].

STEP 7 Allow to cool in the tin for 5 minutes before slicing into squares and serving warm, or allow to cool completely in the tin. **MAKES 16**

NOTE
+ *The brownie is ready when the top feels set to the touch.*

TIPS
If you're not serving the brownie warm, let it cool in the tin, then turn out and slice into squares. It'll continue to set in the tin, but stay soft and fudgy in the centre.
The two types of sugar in these brownies work their magic in different ways. Caster sugar lends sweetness and helps create a smooth and crispy top. Brown sugar adds to the rich, moist centre.
Brownies will keep in an airtight container for up to 1 week.

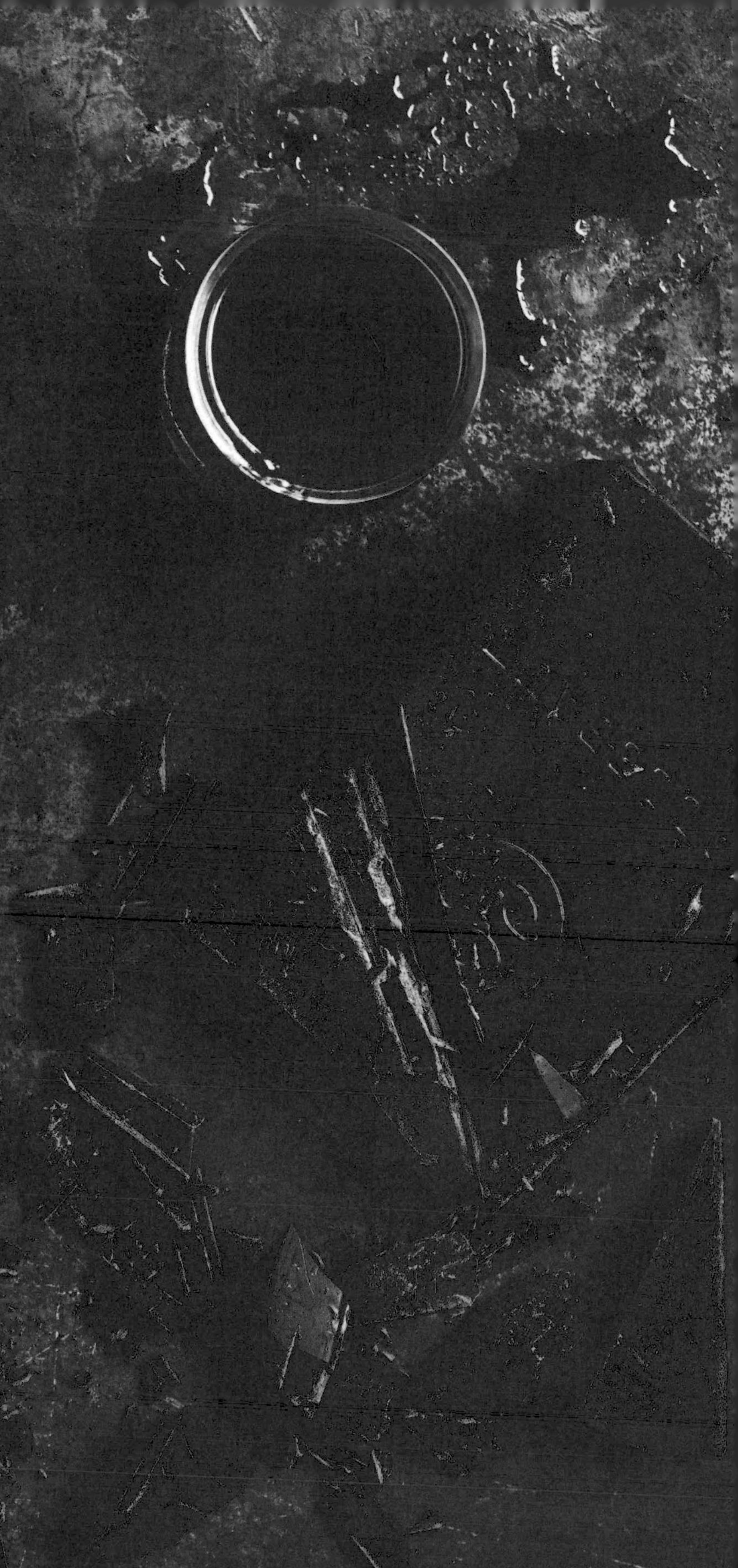

peanut butter swirl brownies + salted caramel brownies

fudgy chocolate puddings with raspberries

peanut butter swirl brownies

½ cup (140g) smooth peanut butter, softened
1 x quantity molten choc-chunk brownie mixture
   (see *basic recipe*)[+]

Preheat oven to 160°C (325°F). Spoon the peanut butter
over the brownie mixture and swirl through, using a
butter knife. Bake for 50 minutes – 1 hour or until the
brownie is set. Allow to cool in the tin for 5 minutes
before slicing into squares and serving warm, or allow
to cool completely in the tin. **MAKES 16**

NOTE
*+ This recipe begins with uncooked
brownie mixture – simply prepare
the basic recipe until the end of step 5.*

salted caramel brownies

140g store-bought caramel fudge, roughly chopped
1 x quantity molten choc-chunk brownie mixture
   (see *basic recipe*)[+]
1 teaspoon sea salt flakes

Preheat oven to 160°C (325°F). Sprinkle the fudge over
the brownie mixture, pressing in gently. Sprinkle with
the salt. Bake for 50 minutes – 1 hour or until the brownie
is set. Allow to cool in the tin for 5 minutes before slicing
into squares and serving warm, or allow to cool completely
in the tin. **MAKES 16**

NOTE
*+ This recipe begins with uncooked
brownie mixture – simply prepare
the basic recipe until the end of step 5.*

fudgy chocolate puddings with raspberries

1 x quantity molten choc-chunk brownie mixture
   (see *basic recipe*)[+]
175g raspberries

Preheat oven to 160°C (325°F). Lightly grease
12 x ½-cup-capacity (125ml) muffin tins. Divide
the brownie mixture between the tins and top each
with the raspberries, pressing in gently. Bake for
35–40 minutes or until the puddings are just set.
Turn out onto serving plates and serve warm. **MAKES 12**

NOTE
*+ This recipe begins with uncooked
brownie mixture – simply prepare
the basic recipe until the end of step 2.*
TIP
*Perfect as individual desserts, serve
warm puddings with double cream.*

cheesecake ripple brownies

1 x quantity molten choc-chunk brownie mixture
   (see *basic recipe*)[+]
250g cream cheese, softened
1 teaspoon vanilla extract
1 egg

Preheat oven to 150°C (300°F). Lightly grease and
line a 20cm square tin with non-stick baking paper.
Spread the brownie mixture into the tin.
   Place the cream cheese, vanilla and egg in the bowl
of an electric mixer and beat on low speed until smooth.
Spoon the cream cheese mixture over the brownie
mixture and swirl through, using a butter knife. Bake for
1 hour 10 minutes – 1 hour 20 minutes or until the
brownie is set. Allow to cool in the tin for 5 minutes
before slicing into squares and serving warm, or allow
to cool completely in the tin. **MAKES 16**

NOTE
*+ This recipe begins with uncooked
brownie mixture – simply prepare
the basic recipe until the end of step 2.*

cheesecake ripple brownies

the basic

VANILLA SNAP BISCUITS

VANILLA SNAP BISCUITS

185g unsalted butter, chopped

1 cup (220g) caster (superfine) sugar

1½ teaspoons vanilla extract

2½ cups (375g) plain (all-purpose) flour

1 egg

1 egg yolk, extra

STEP 1 Place the butter, sugar and vanilla in a food processor and process until smooth.

STEP 2 Add the flour, egg and extra egg yolk and process until a smooth dough forms.

STEP 3 Turn the dough out onto a lightly floured surface and divide in half.

STEP 4 Roll each piece out between sheets of non-stick baking paper until 5mm thick.

STEP 5 Refrigerate for 10 minutes or until firm.

STEP 6 Preheat oven to 160°C (325°F).

STEP 7 Remove the top sheets of baking paper from the dough. Using a 6cm round cookie cutter, cut shapes from the dough, re-rolling as necessary.

STEP 8 Place the rounds on lightly greased baking trays lined with non-stick baking paper and bake for 12–14 minutes or until golden.

STEP 9 Allow to cool on trays for 10 minutes before transferring onto wire racks to cool. **MAKES 44**

simple vanilla jam drops

caramel cookie sandwiches

sweetheart biscuits

simple vanilla jam drops

1 x quantity unrolled vanilla snap biscuit dough
  (see *basic recipe*)[+]
½ cup (160g) raspberry jam

Preheat oven to 180°C (350°F). Roll tablespoons of the
dough into balls and place on lightly greased baking trays
lined with non-stick baking paper. Flatten slightly and,
using your fingertip, make an indent in each round.
Fill each indent with ½ teaspoon of the jam. Bake for
12–14 minutes or until golden. Allow to cool on trays for
10 minutes before transferring onto wire racks to cool
completely. **MAKES 30**

NOTE
+ This recipe begins with unrolled
biscuit dough – simply prepare the
basic recipe until the end of step 2.

caramel cookie sandwiches

1 x quantity rolled vanilla snap biscuit dough
  (see *basic recipe*)[+]
1 cup (320g) creamy caramel (see *basic recipe*, page 264)
  or store-bought caramel

Preheat oven to 160°C (325°F). Remove the top sheets of
baking paper from the dough. Using a fluted 6cm square
cookie cutter, cut shapes from the dough, re-rolling as
necessary. Place on lightly greased baking trays lined with
non-stick baking paper. Bake for 12–14 minutes or until
golden. Allow to cool on trays for 10 minutes before
transferring onto wire racks to cool completely.
  Spread 1 tablespoon of the caramel onto each of 22 of
the cookies. Sandwich with the remaining cookies. **MAKES 22**

NOTE
+ This recipe begins with rolled
biscuit dough – simply prepare the
basic recipe until the end of step 5.

sweetheart biscuits

1 x quantity rolled vanilla snap biscuit dough
  (see *basic recipe*)[+]
sanding sugar* or white (granulated) sugar, for sprinkling

Preheat oven to 160°C (325°F). Remove the top sheets of
baking paper from the dough. Using a 6cm heart-shaped
cookie cutter, cut shapes from the dough, re-rolling as
necessary. Place on lightly greased baking trays lined with
non-stick baking paper. Sprinkle with sugar and bake for
12–14 minutes or until golden. Allow to cool on trays for
10 minutes before transferring onto wire racks to cool.
MAKES 44

NOTE
+ This recipe begins with rolled
biscuit dough – simply prepare the
basic recipe until the end of step 5.

the basic

BANANA BREAD

BANANA BREAD

1½ cups (390g) mashed ripe banana (about 4 bananas)⁺

½ cup (125ml) vegetable oil or
light-flavoured extra virgin olive oil

3 eggs

1½ cups (260g) brown sugar

1 teaspoon vanilla extract

1½ cups (225g) self-raising (self-rising) flour

1 teaspoon ground cinnamon

1 banana, extra, halved lengthways

STEP 1 Place the mashed banana in a large bowl. Add the oil, eggs, sugar and vanilla and mix to combine.

STEP 2 Add the flour and cinnamon and mix until just combined[++].

STEP 3 Preheat oven to 180°C (350°F).

STEP 4 Lightly grease a 10cm x 20cm (2-litre-capacity) loaf tin and line with non-stick baking paper[+++].

STEP 5 Pour the banana mixture into the tin and top with the extra banana, cut side up.

STEP 6 Bake for 1 hour or until cooked when tested with a skewer. Allow to cool in the tin for 5 minutes before placing onto a wire rack to cool completely. Slice to serve. **SERVES 8–10**

NOTES

+ Ripe bananas lend a lovely natural sweetness to the bread.

++ **It's best not to overwork the mixture – just mix until the ingredients are combined.**

+++ When lining the tin, leave a few centimetres of baking paper overhanging at each long edge. You can use these to help lift the baked banana bread out from the tin and onto the cooling rack.

easy banana muffins

banana bundt cake with caramel icing

easy banana muffins

1 x quantity banana bread mixture (see *basic recipe*)[+]
demerara sugar, for sprinkling
maple syrup, to serve

Preheat oven to 180°C (350°F). Line 12 x ½-cup-capacity
(125ml) muffin tins with paper cases. Divide the banana
mixture between the tins. Top with the extra banana
and sprinkle with sugar. Bake for 16–18 minutes or until
cooked when tested with a skewer. Turn out onto a wire
rack to cool. Drizzle with maple syrup to serve[++]. **MAKES 12**

NOTES
*+ This recipe begins with uncooked
banana bread mixture – simply
prepare the basic recipe until the
end of step 2, chopping the extra
banana and keeping it on-hand
to top each muffin.*
*++ **For lunchbox-ready muffins,
you can omit the maple syrup.***

banana bundt cake with caramel icing

1 x quantity banana bread mixture (see *basic recipe*)[+]
1 cup (320g) creamy caramel (see *basic recipe*, page 264)
    or store-bought caramel

Preheat oven to 180°C (350°F). Grease a 24cm Bundt
cake tin[++]. Pour the banana mixture into the tin.
Bake for 40–45 minutes or until cooked when tested
with a skewer. Immediately turn out onto a wire
rack to cool completely. Refrigerate until chilled.
    Place the cake on a cake stand or plate and top
with the caramel. Slice to serve. **SERVES 8**

NOTES
*+ This recipe begins with uncooked
banana bread mixture – simply
prepare the basic recipe until the end
of step 2, omitting the extra banana.*
*++ **Grease the Bundt tin well,
with butter or cooking oil spray.***
TIPS
*Spooning the caramel over the
chilled cake will help it set into
a sweet golden icing.*
***You can also top slices of
the cake with warm caramel
and double cream, for a cosy
pudding-style dessert.***

MY NAN'S SPONGE CAKE

MY NAN'S SPONGE CAKE

1 cup (150g) plain (all-purpose) flour

1 teaspoon baking powder

6 eggs

3/4 cup (165g) caster (superfine) sugar

1 teaspoon vanilla extract

75g unsalted butter, melted

STEP 1 Preheat oven to 160°C (325°F).

STEP 2 Lightly grease 2 x 20cm round cake tins and line with non-stick baking paper.

STEP 3 Sift the flour and baking powder together 3 times and set aside.

STEP 4 Place the eggs, sugar and vanilla in the bowl of an electric mixer and whisk on high speed for 12–15 minutes or until pale, thick and tripled in volume.

STEP 5 Sift half the flour mixture into the egg mixture and, using a large metal spoon, gently fold to combine[+]. Repeat with the remaining flour mixture.

STEP 6 Add the butter and gently fold to combine.

STEP 7 Divide the mixture between the prepared tins and gently smooth the tops, using a palette knife[++].

STEP 8 Bake for 20–25 minutes or until the cakes are springy to the touch and come away from the sides of the tins. Turn out onto wire racks covered with clean tea towels and allow to cool completely. **MAKES 1 QUANTITY**

NOTES
+ Use a large metal spoon to combine the flour and egg mixtures, with a gentle cutting, lifting and folding action.
*++ **Be gentle when smoothing the tops of the cakes, to keep the mixture light and airy.***
TIP
By covering the cooling racks with tea towels (or non-stick baking paper), you'll prevent the wire from imprinting grid marks on the cakes.

italian ricotta sponge cake

italian ricotta sponge cake

1 x quantity my nan's sponge cake (see *basic recipe*)
1 x quantity mascarpone icing (see *basic recipe*, page 225)
ricotta filling
1½ cups (360g) fresh ricotta
¼ cup (40g) icing (confectioner's) sugar, sifted
1 teaspoon finely grated lemon rind
1 tablespoon lemon juice

To make the ricotta filling, place the ricotta, sugar, lemon rind and juice in the bowl of an electric mixer and beat on low speed for 2 minutes or until smooth. Set aside.

To assemble the cake, place one of the sponge cakes on a cake stand or plate. Spread with the ricotta filling and top with the remaining cake. Using a palette knife, spread the top and sides of the cake with the mascarpone icing. Slice to serve. **SERVES 8-10**

TIP
Simple and elegant, this is a perfect cake for celebrations like birthdays and baby showers. It's equally pretty piled with berries or topped with garden roses (choose pesticide-free) for something special.

dark chocolate lamingtons

1 x quantity my nan's sponge cake mixture (see *basic recipe*)[+]
½ x quantity dark chocolate ganache
    (see *basic recipe*, page 232)
½ cup (160g) raspberry jam
3 cups (150g) coconut flakes[*]

Preheat oven to 160°C (325°F). Lightly grease a 20cm x 30cm slice tin and line with non-stick baking paper. Pour the cake mixture into the tin and bake for 20–25 minutes or until the cake is springy to the touch and comes away from the sides of the tin. Turn out onto a wire rack covered with a clean tea towel and allow to cool completely.

Using a serrated knife, cut the cake in half horizontally. Spread one half with ½ cup (125ml) of the ganache. Spread the remaining cake half with the jam. Sandwich together and refrigerate for 10 minutes or until the ganache is firm.

Cut the cake into 5cm squares. Using a butter knife, spread the squares with the remaining ganache to coat. Sprinkle with the coconut and place on a tray lined with non-stick baking paper. Refrigerate until firm. Place on a cake stand or plate to serve. **MAKES 24**

NOTE
+ This recipe begins with uncooked sponge cake mixture – simply prepare the basic recipe until the end of step 6, swapping the 2 round cake tins for a slice tin, as above.

dark chocolate lamingtons

individual tiramisu trifles

individual tiramisu trifles

1 x quantity my nan's sponge cake (see *basic recipe*)
2 cups (500g) mascarpone*
2 cups (500ml) single (pouring) cream*
⅓ cup (55g) icing (confectioner's) sugar, sifted
8 x 30ml shots espresso[+]
⅓ cup (80ml) sweet sherry
1 teaspoon vanilla extract
Dutch cocoa*, for dusting

Using a serrated knife, cut the sponge cakes in half horizontally. Using a cookie cutter, cut 12 rounds from the cake to fit snugly into 6 x 1½-cup-capacity (375ml) glasses.

Place the mascarpone, cream and sugar in the bowl of an electric mixer and whisk until soft peaks form. Set aside.

Place the espresso, sherry and vanilla in a medium bowl and stir to combine. Set aside.

To assemble the trifles, place 1 round of cake in the base of each glass. Top each with 1 tablespoon of the coffee mixture and ⅓ cup (80ml) of the mascarpone mixture. Repeat the layering once more and refrigerate for a minimum of 30 minutes. Dust with cocoa to serve. **MAKES 6**

NOTE
+ If you don't have access to an espresso machine, use 1 cup (250ml) strong brewed or percolated coffee instead.
TIP
You can use coffee-flavoured liqueur or marsala in place of the sherry.

raspberry and cream layered sponge cake

1 x quantity my nan's sponge cake (see *basic recipe*)
2 cups (500ml) single (pouring) cream*
¼ cup (40g) icing (confectioner's) sugar, sifted
1 teaspoon vanilla extract
1 cup (320g) raspberry jam
375g raspberries

Using a serrated knife, cut the sponge cakes in half horizontally and set aside.

Place the cream, sugar and vanilla in the bowl of an electric mixer and whisk until soft peaks form. Set aside.

To assemble the cake, place a base layer of sponge cake, cut-side up, on a cake stand or plate. Spread with ¼ cup (80g) of the jam and ¾ cup (180ml) of the cream mixture. Sprinkle with one-quarter of the raspberries. Repeat twice more and top with a final layer of sponge, cut-side down. Spoon the remaining cream mixture onto the cake and swirl through the remaining jam. Sprinkle with the remaining raspberries to serve. **SERVES 8–10**

TIPS
This luscious cake can also be layered with fresh strawberries or blueberries. ***Choose your favourite fruit jam to spread on each layer and swirl on top.*** *It's a good idea to use the measurements given when spreading the jam and cream. It makes for even layers and a stable cake.*

raspberry and cream layered sponge cake

SIMPLE MUFFIN MIXTURE

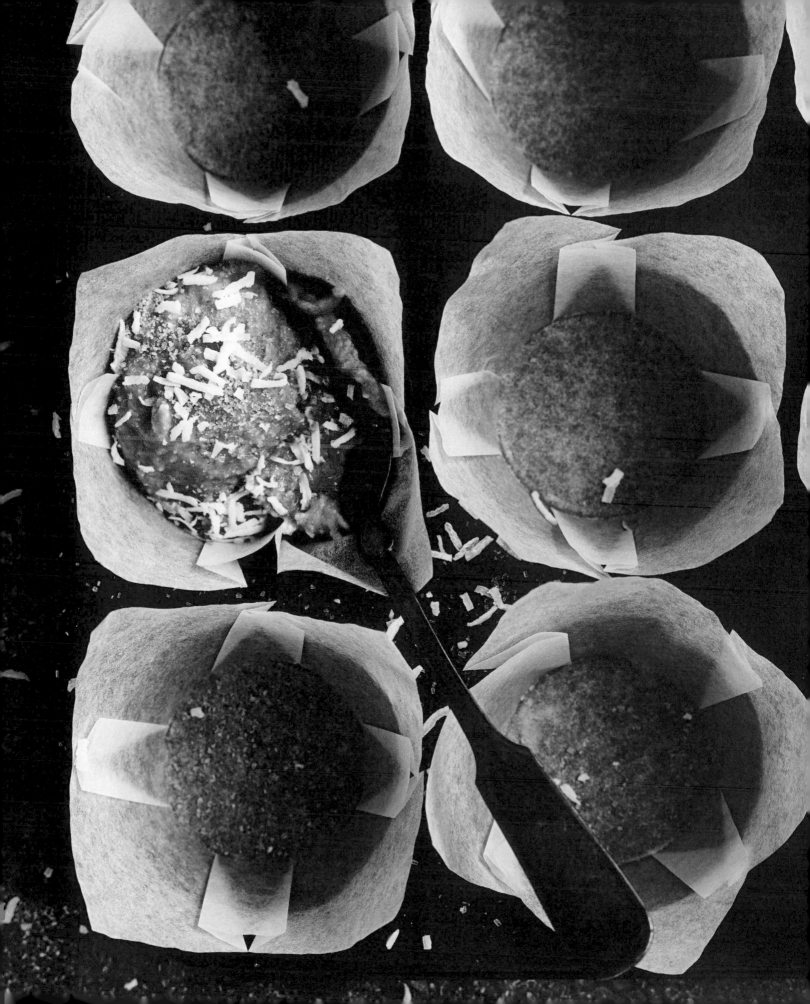

SIMPLE MUFFIN MIXTURE

2½ cups (375g) self-raising (self-rising) flour

1 teaspoon baking powder

1 cup (220g) raw caster (superfine) sugar⁺

1 egg

½ cup (125ml) vegetable oil or light-flavoured extra virgin olive oil

2 teaspoons vanilla extract

¾ cup (180ml) milk

STEP 1 Place the flour, baking powder and sugar in a large bowl and mix to combine.

STEP 2 Place the egg, oil, vanilla and milk in a medium bowl and whisk to combine.

STEP 3 Add the egg mixture to the flour mixture and fold until almost combined⁺⁺.

MAKES 1 QUANTITY

—

NOTES
+ *Raw caster sugar has a honey-caramel flavour, making it perfect for baking. If unavailable, use regular caster sugar.*
++ **See the recipes that follow for how to bake this mixture into muffins.**

banana and coconut muffins

date and cinnamon muffins

raspberry and white chocolate muffins

carrot cake and cream cheese muffins

banana and coconut muffins

3 cups (780g) roughly mashed banana (about 8 bananas)
1¼ cups (100g) shredded coconut*
1 x quantity simple muffin mixture (see *basic recipe*)
1 tablespoon raw caster (superfine) sugar

Preheat oven to 180°C (350°F). Line 12 x ½-cup-capacity
(125ml) muffin tins with paper cases and set aside.

Add the banana and ¾ cup (60g) of the coconut to
the muffin mixture and fold until just combined. Divide
the mixture between the prepared tins. Place the sugar
and the remaining coconut in a small bowl and mix to
combine. Sprinkle the muffins with the coconut sugar
and bake for 25–30 minutes or until cooked when tested
with a skewer. Transfer to a wire rack to cool. **MAKES 12**

date and cinnamon muffins

2 cups (460g) fresh dates, pitted and finely chopped
3 teaspoons ground cinnamon
1 x quantity simple muffin mixture (see *basic recipe*)
1 tablespoon raw caster (superfine) sugar

Preheat oven to 180°C (350°F). Line 12 x ½-cup-capacity
(125ml) muffin tins with paper cases and set aside.

Add the date and 2 teaspoons of the cinnamon to the
muffin mixture and mix until just combined. Divide
the mixture between the prepared tins. Place the sugar
and the remaining cinnamon in a small bowl and mix to
combine. Sprinkle the muffins with the cinnamon sugar
and bake for 20–25 minutes or until cooked when tested
with a skewer. Transfer to a wire rack to cool. **MAKES 12**

TIPS
*Sprinkling muffins with sugar before they're
baked gives them a crunchy golden crust.*
**Muffins freeze well – once cool, wrap
them in plastic wrap and freeze. Thaw
for lunchboxes or easy afternoon tea.**

raspberry and white chocolate muffins

3 cups (390g) frozen raspberries
180g white chocolate, chopped
1 x quantity simple muffin mixture (see *basic recipe*)

Preheat oven to 180°C (350°F). Line 12 x ½-cup-capacity
(125ml) muffin tins with paper cases and set aside.

Add the raspberries and chocolate to the muffin mixture
and mix until just combined. Divide the mixture between
the prepared tins. Bake for 25–30 minutes or until cooked
when tested with a skewer. Transfer to a wire rack to cool.
MAKES 12

TIP
*You can swap the raspberries for blueberries
here – frozen berries work well as they hold
their shape. You could also try using chopped
apple or firm pear.*

carrot cake and cream cheese muffins

250g cream cheese, softened
1 tablespoon raw caster (superfine) sugar
3 carrots (450g), peeled and grated
2 teaspoons ground cinnamon
1 cup (100g) walnuts, chopped
1 x quantity simple muffin mixture (see *basic recipe*)

Preheat oven to 180°C (350°F). Line 12 x ½-cup-capacity
(125ml) muffin tins with paper cases and set aside.

Place the cream cheese and sugar in a medium bowl
and mix until smooth. Set aside.

Add the carrot, cinnamon and walnut to the muffin
mixture and mix until just combined. Divide half the
mixture between the prepared tins. Place 1 heaped
tablespoon of the cream cheese mixture onto each
muffin. Top with the remaining muffin mixture and
bake for 20–25 minutes or until cooked when tested
with a skewer. Transfer to a wire rack to cool. **MAKES 12**

———

BAKED RICOTTA CHEESECAKE

BAKED RICOTTA CHEESECAKE

base

1 cup (150g) plain (all-purpose) flour

¼ cup (55g) caster (superfine) sugar

100g unsalted butter, chopped

filling

330g cream cheese, chopped and softened

500g fresh ricotta

1⅓ cups (295g) caster (superfine) sugar

¼ cup (60ml) lemon juice

2 tablespoons finely grated lemon rind

1 teaspoon vanilla extract

1 tablespoon cornflour (cornstarch)

1 tablespoon water

5 eggs

STEP 1 Preheat oven to 150°C (300°F).

STEP 2 Lightly grease a 22cm round springform cake tin and line the base with non-stick baking paper. Set aside.

STEP 3 To make the base, place the flour, sugar and butter in a food processor and process for 1 minute or until a rough dough forms.

STEP 4 Using the back of a spoon, press the mixture into the base of the prepared tin. Bake for 30–35 minutes or until golden and just cooked. Set aside to cool slightly.

STEP 5 While the base is baking, make the filling. Place the cream cheese, ricotta, sugar, lemon juice, lemon rind and vanilla in a food processor and process until smooth. Place the cornflour and water in a small bowl and mix until smooth. Add the cornflour mixture and the eggs to the filling and process to combine.

STEP 6 Lightly re-grease the sides of the cake tin and pour the filling over the base, tapping gently to remove any air bubbles.

STEP 7 Bake for 50 minutes – 1 hour or until light golden and just set. Allow to cool in the closed oven for 50 minutes.

STEP 8 Refrigerate for 1 hour or until chilled. Remove the cheesecake from the tin and place on a cake stand or plate to serve. **SERVES 8–10**

raspberry swirl cheesecake

lemon cheesecake

1/2 cups (195g) frozen raspberries, thawed
½ cup (110g) caster (superfine) sugar
1 x quantity baked ricotta cheesecake (see *basic recipe*),
    filling uncooked[+]

Place the raspberries in a small food processor and process
until smooth. Strain through a fine sieve into a small
saucepan, discarding any solids. Place over high heat
and add the sugar. Bring to a simmer, stirring until the
sugar has dissolved. Cook for 3 minutes or until thickened
slightly. Allow to cool to room temperature.

Preheat oven to 150°C (300°F). Pour the raspberry syrup
onto the cheesecake and gently swirl through the filling,
using a butter knife. Bake for 50 minutes – 1 hour or until
light golden and just set. Allow to cool in the closed oven
for 50 minutes. Refrigerate for 1 hour or until chilled.

Remove the cheesecake from the tin and place on a cake
stand or plate to serve. **SERVES 8-10**

NOTE
*+ This recipe begins with just-filled
cheesecake (filling not yet baked).
Simply prepare the basic recipe
until the end of step 6.*

½ x quantity classic lemon curd (see *basic recipe*, page 286)
    or ¾ cup (240g) store-bought lemon curd
1 x quantity baked ricotta cheesecake (see *basic recipe*)

Spread the lemon curd over the cheesecake to serve.
SERVES 8-10

TIP
*The cheesecake has a little lemon in the
filling, giving it a lovely hint of tartness.
When topped with the velvety sweet curd,
the flavours truly sing.*

ricotta cheesecake with almond praline

1 x quantity baked ricotta cheesecake (see *basic recipe*)
almond praline
¾ cup (165g) raw caster (superfine) sugar[+]
½ cup (40g) flaked almonds, toasted

To make the almond praline, preheat oven to 200°C (400°F).
Sprinkle the sugar over a large lightly greased baking tray
lined with non-stick baking paper. Bake for 12–15 minutes
or until melted. Sprinkle with the almonds and allow to set
completely on the tray. Crush the praline into small pieces.

Sprinkle the cheesecake with the almond praline to serve,
pressing gently to secure. **SERVES 8-10**

NOTE
*+ Raw caster sugar is light golden in
colour with a honey-caramel flavour,
making it perfect for this praline. If
unavailable, use regular caster sugar.*
TIP
*For a finer praline crust, place broken
praline in a small food processor and
process until finely chopped. Sprinkle
evenly over the cheesecake to serve.*

ricotta cheesecake with almond praline

LIGHT AND
FLUFFY PANCAKES

LIGHT AND FLUFFY PANCAKES

¾ cup (110g) self-raising (self-rising) flour

1 teaspoon baking powder

⅓ cup (75g) caster (superfine) sugar

¾ cup (180ml) buttermilk*

2 eggs, separated

STEP 1 Place the flour, baking powder, sugar, buttermilk and egg yolks in a large bowl and whisk until a smooth batter forms.

STEP 2 Place the eggwhites in the bowl of an electric mixer and whisk on high speed until stiff peaks form.

STEP 3 Add the eggwhite to the pancake batter and gently fold to combine.

STEP 4 Place a large non-stick frying pan over medium heat.

STEP 5 In batches, cook heaped tablespoons of the mixture for 3–4 minutes each side or until golden brown. **MAKES 12**

TIPS

Gently folding in the whisked eggwhite will keep these pancakes super light.
Buttermilk makes them extra fluffy.
Serve pancakes hot from the pan or stack on a warm plate and cover with a tea towel until you've cooked the batch.
Drizzle with maple syrup to serve.

blueberry pancakes with whipped ricotta and lemon curd

ricotta pancakes with lemon and sugar

blueberry pancakes with whipped ricotta and lemon curd

1 cup (240g) fresh ricotta
½ cup (160g) classic lemon curd (see *basic recipe*, page 286)
  or store-bought lemon curd
125g blueberries, lightly crushed
1 x quantity light and fluffy pancake mixture
  (see *basic recipe*)[+]

Place the ricotta in a small food processor and process until smooth. Transfer to a small bowl and add the lemon curd. Swirl to combine and set aside.

Add the blueberries to the pancake mixture and gently fold to combine. Place a large non-stick frying pan over medium heat. In batches, cook heaped tablespoons of the mixture for 3–4 minutes each side or until golden brown. Serve with the whipped ricotta and lemon curd. **MAKES 12**

NOTE
+ This recipe begins with uncooked pancake mixture – simply prepare the basic recipe until the end of step 3.

ricotta pancakes with lemon and sugar

1 teaspoon finely grated lemon rind
1 cup (240g) fresh ricotta
1 x quantity light and fluffy pancake mixture
  (see *basic recipe*), whisked eggwhites still separate[+]
caster (superfine) sugar, for sprinkling
2 lemons, cut into wedges

Add the lemon rind and ricotta to the pancake batter and stir to combine. Add the eggwhite and gently fold to combine.

Place a large non-stick frying pan over medium heat. In batches, cook heaped tablespoons of the mixture for 3–4 minutes each side or until golden brown. Sprinkle with sugar and serve with the lemon wedges. **MAKES 16**

NOTE
+ This recipe begins with uncooked pancake mixture – simply prepare the basic recipe until the end of step 2.

mini pancakes in cinnamon sugar

1 x quantity light and fluffy pancake mixture
  (see *basic recipe*)[+]
¾ teaspoon ground cinnamon
¼ cup (55g) caster (superfine) sugar
25g unsalted butter, melted

Place a large non-stick frying pan over medium heat. In batches, cook heaped teaspoons of the pancake mixture for 1–2 minutes each side or until golden brown.

Place the cinnamon and sugar in a small bowl and mix to combine. Place the pancakes and butter in a large bowl and toss to combine. Add the cinnamon sugar and toss to coat. Place on a serving plate and sprinkle with any remaining cinnamon sugar to serve. **MAKES 60**

NOTE
+ This recipe begins with uncooked pancake mixture – simply prepare the basic recipe until the end of step 3.

mini pancakes in cinnamon sugar

the basic

—

CLASSIC VANILLA CUSTARD

CLASSIC VANILLA CUSTARD

1 litre single (pouring) cream*

2 vanilla beans, split and seeds scraped

10 egg yolks

¾ cup (165g) caster (superfine) sugar

STEP 1 Place the cream, vanilla beans and seeds in a medium saucepan over medium heat and bring to a simmer⁺. Remove from the heat and set aside.

STEP 2 Place the egg yolks and sugar in a large bowl and whisk until pale and thick.

STEP 3 Gradually add the vanilla cream to the egg mixture, reserving the vanilla beans, and whisk continuously until combined.

STEP 4 Return the mixture to the cleaned saucepan with the vanilla beans and place over medium heat. Cook, stirring, for 14–16 minutes or until the custard has thickened and coats the back of a spoon.

STEP 5 Strain into a heatproof bowl and discard any solids. **MAKES 1 LITRE**

NOTE
+ The vanilla cream is simmering when bubbles begin to form around the edges.

TIPS
To chill the custard, cover its surface completely with plastic wrap and place in the refrigerator. Allowing the plastic wrap to touch the custard will prevent a skin from forming.
Store the custard, covered as above, for 1–2 days in the refrigerator.
For a sweet and delicious way to use up spare eggwhites, see the no-fail meringue mixture recipe on page 240.

old-fashioned vanilla slice

raspberry semifreddo

old-fashioned vanilla slice

2 sheets (750g) store-bought butter puff pastry*, thawed
2 tablespoons cornflour (cornstarch)
1 tablespoon water
1 x quantity classic vanilla custard (see *basic recipe*),
   heated through
lemon icing
1½ cups (240g) icing (confectioner's) sugar, sifted
2 tablespoons lemon juice

Preheat oven to 200°C (400°F). Place each pastry sheet
on a lightly greased baking tray lined with non-stick
baking paper. Top each with non-stick baking paper and
weigh down with another baking tray. Bake, swapping
the shelf positions of the trays halfway through cooking
time, for 22–25 minutes or until golden. Transfer the
pastry to wire racks to cool completely.

Line a lightly greased 22cm square cake tin with
non-stick baking paper⁺. Using a serrated knife, trim
the pastry sheets to fit the tin. Place 1 pastry square in
the base of the tin.

Place the cornflour and water in a small bowl and mix
to combine. Place the hot custard in a medium saucepan
over medium heat. Add the cornflour mixture and cook,
stirring, for 1 minute or until thickened. Pour the custard
mixture into the prepared tin, top with the remaining
pastry square and press gently to secure. Refrigerate for
3–4 hours or until set.

To make the lemon icing, place the sugar and lemon juice
in a medium bowl and mix to combine.

Lift the slice from the tin and place on a serving tray.
Spoon over the icing and allow to set. Slice into bars to
serve. **SERVES 6–8**

NOTE
*+ When lining the cake tin, leave a few
centimetres of baking paper overhanging
at the sides. These will help you lift the
slice from the tin once it's chilled.*

raspberry semifreddo

1½ cups (375ml) single (pouring) cream*
½ cup (80g) icing (confectioner's) sugar, sifted
1 x quantity classic vanilla custard (see *basic recipe*),
   cooled to room temperature
2 cups (260g) frozen raspberries

Lightly grease a 2-litre-capacity loaf tin and line with
non-stick baking paper. Set aside.

Place the cream and sugar in the bowl of an electric
mixer and whisk until soft peaks form. Add the custard
and fold to combine. Add the raspberries and gently fold
to combine. Pour into the prepared tin, cover with plastic
wrap and freeze for 6 hours or overnight until solid.

Turn out onto a serving plate and slice to serve. **SERVES 6–8**

vanilla bean ice-cream with pistachio praline

1 x quantity classic vanilla custard (see *basic recipe*),
   cooled to room temperature
waffle cones, to serve
1 x quantity pistachio praline (see *basic recipe*, page 225)

Pour the custard into a large zip-lock plastic bag
and gently press out any air. Freeze for 3–4 hours
or overnight until solid.

Break the ice-cream into small pieces and place in
a food processor⁺. Process until smooth and pour into
a 1-litre-capacity metal container. Freeze for 3 hours
or overnight until solid.

Scoop the ice-cream into cones and top with the
praline to serve. **MAKES 1 LITRE**

NOTE
*+ To break the ice-cream up into small
pieces, you can bend it and tap it on your
benchtop while it's still in the zip-lock
bag. Then simply unseal and empty into
the food processor.*

vanilla bean ice-cream with pistachio praline

the basic

ONE-BOWL VANILLA CAKE

ONE-BOWL VANILLA CAKE

125g unsalted butter, melted and cooled

1½ cups (225g) self-raising (self-rising) flour, sifted

1 cup (220g) caster (superfine) sugar

2 teaspoons vanilla extract

½ teaspoon baking powder

2 eggs

½ cup (125ml) milk

STEP 1 Place the butter, flour, sugar, vanilla, baking powder, eggs and milk in a large bowl and whisk until well combined.

STEP 2 Preheat oven to 160°C (325°F).

STEP 3 Lightly grease a 20cm round cake tin and line with non-stick baking paper.

STEP 4 Pour the mixture into the tin, smooth the top and bake for 55 minutes – 1 hour or until cooked when tested with a skewer.

STEP 5 Allow to cool in the tin for 5 minutes before turning out onto a wire rack to cool completely. Slice to serve. **SERVES 8**

peach, raspberry and vanilla tray cake

vanilla cupcakes with white chocolate frosting

vanilla heart cakes with rosewater icing

1 x quantity one-bowl vanilla cake mixture (see *basic recipe*)[+]
4 yellow peaches (500g), sliced
125g raspberries

Preheat oven to 160°C (325°F). Lightly grease a 20cm x 30cm slice tin and line with non-stick baking paper. Spread the cake mixture into the tin. Top with the peach and raspberries, pressing down gently. Bake for 50–55 minutes or until cooked when tested with a skewer. Allow to cool completely in the tin before slicing to serve. **SERVES 8**

NOTE
+ *This recipe begins with uncooked cake mixture. Simply prepare the basic recipe until the end of step 1.*
TIP
Swap nectarines, plums or any summer berries you like into this rustic afternoon tea cake.

vanilla cupcakes with white chocolate frosting

1 x quantity one-bowl vanilla cake mixture (see *basic recipe*)[+]
¾ cup (180ml) single (pouring) cream*
375g white chocolate, grated or finely chopped
2 teaspoons vanilla bean paste

Preheat oven to 160°C (325°F). Line 18 x ½-cup-capacity (125ml) muffin tins with paper cases. Spoon the cake mixture into the tins and bake for 20–25 minutes or until cooked when tested with a skewer. Transfer to wire racks to cool completely.
　Place the cream in a small saucepan over low heat. Cook, stirring occasionally, until hot but not boiling. Place the chocolate in a large bowl and add the cream. Stir once to remove any chocolate from the base of the bowl and set aside for 2 minutes. Stir the ganache gently until just combined. Refrigerate until just cool. Add the vanilla and whisk until soft peaks form. Spoon the frosting into a piping bag fitted with a 1cm plain nozzle and pipe onto each cupcake to serve. **MAKES 18**

NOTE
+ *This recipe begins with uncooked cake mixture. Simply prepare the basic recipe until the end of step 1.*

1 x quantity one-bowl vanilla cake mixture (see *basic recipe*)[+]
2 cups (320g) icing (confectioner's) sugar, sifted
¼ teaspoon rosewater*
¼ cup (60ml) boiling water
edible dried rose petals*, for sprinkling

Preheat oven to 160°C (325°F). Lightly grease a 20cm x 30cm slice tin and line with non-stick baking paper. Spread the cake mixture into the tin and bake for 35–40 minutes or until cooked when tested with a skewer. Allow to cool in the tin for 5 minutes. Turn out onto a wire rack to cool completely.
　Place the sugar, rosewater and water in a large bowl and whisk until smooth. Use an 8cm heart-shaped cookie cutter to cut hearts from the cake. Spoon over the icing and top with petals. Refrigerate until just set. **MAKES 8**

NOTE
+ *This recipe begins with uncooked cake mixture. Simply prepare the basic recipe until the end of step 1.*

the basic

SWEET DOUGH

sweet and buttery loaf

SWEET DOUGH

1 teaspoon dry yeast

¼ cup (60ml) warm water

2⅔ cups (400g) plain
(all-purpose) flour

175g unsalted butter, chopped

⅓ cup (75g) caster
(superfine) sugar

2 egg yolks

½ cup (125ml) buttermilk*

1 teaspoon vanilla extract

½ teaspoon table salt

STEP 1 Place the yeast, water and 1 tablespoon of the flour in a small bowl. Mix to combine and set aside.

STEP 2 Place the butter and sugar in the bowl of an electric mixer and beat on low speed until combined.

STEP 3 Increase the speed to medium and beat for 8 minutes or until pale and creamy.

STEP 4 Scrape down the sides of the bowl and add the egg yolks. Beat until well combined.

STEP 5 Reduce the speed to low and gradually add the buttermilk, vanilla, salt, the remaining flour and the yeast mixture and beat until combined.

STEP 6 Scrape down the sides of the bowl. Beat for a further 8–10 minutes or until the dough is smooth.

STEP 7 Turn the dough out onto a lightly floured surface and, kneading gently, bring together.

STEP 8 Transfer to a lightly greased bowl and cover with plastic wrap. Set aside in a warm place for 2–3 hours or until the dough has doubled in size. **MAKES 1 QUANTITY**

sweet

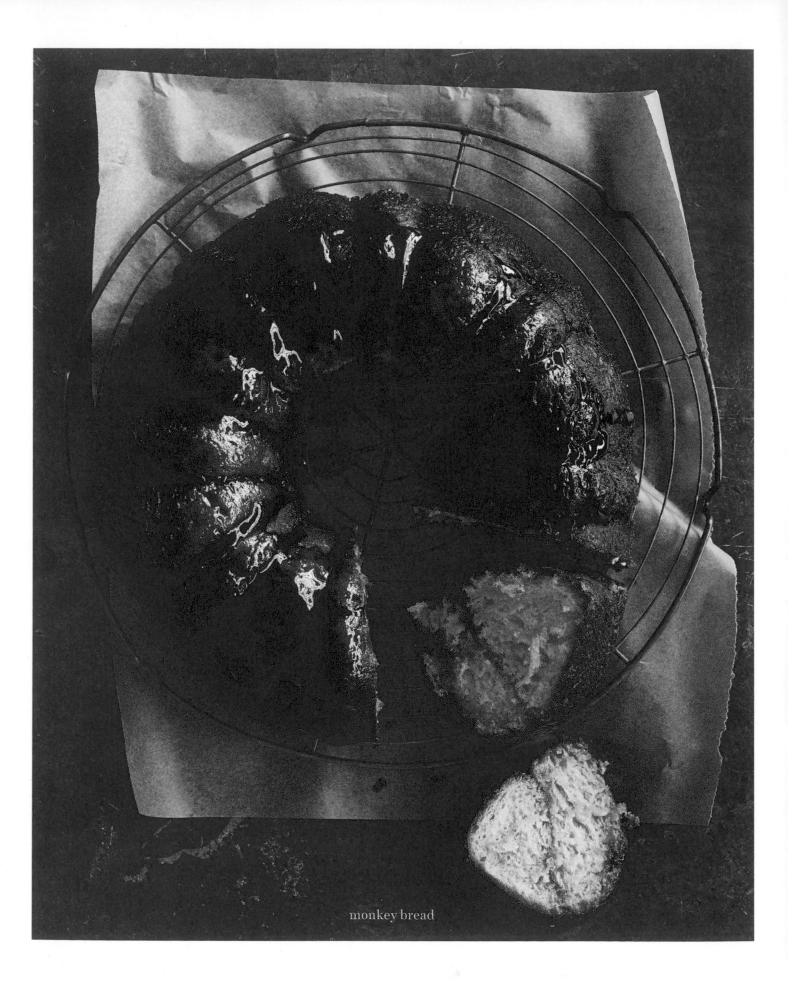

monkey bread

chocolate and hazelnut scrolls

sweet and buttery loaf

25g unsalted butter, melted, plus extra to serve
plain (all-purpose) flour, for dusting
1 x quantity sweet dough (see *basic recipe*)

Brush a 10cm x 20cm (2-litre-capacity) loaf tin with
half the butter. Turn the dough out onto a lightly floured
surface. Divide the dough into 4 equal pieces and shape
into rounds. Arrange in the prepared tin, cover with
plastic wrap and set aside in a warm place for 1–2 hours
or until doubled in size.

Preheat oven to 180°C (350°F). Using kitchen scissors,
snip lengthways down the centre of the dough in the tin
to create 8 portions. Brush the dough with the remaining
butter and bake for 30–35 minutes or until golden. Pull the
loaf apart and spread with extra butter to serve. **SERVES 8**

monkey bread

1 teaspoon ground cinnamon
1 cup (175g) brown sugar
1 x quantity sweet dough (see *basic recipe*)
150g unsalted butter, chopped

Lightly grease a 3-litre-capacity Bundt tin and set aside.

Place the cinnamon and half the sugar in a medium bowl
and mix to combine. Roll heaped tablespoons of the dough
into rounds and toss in the cinnamon sugar to coat.
Arrange the rounds in the prepared tin in 2 layers. Cover
with plastic wrap and set aside in a warm place for 1 hour
or until doubled in size.

Preheat oven to 180°C (350°F). Place the remaining
sugar and the butter in a small saucepan over medium
heat and stir until melted and combined. Pour the butter
mixture over the dough and bake for 30 minutes or until
cooked through and bubbling. Turn out onto a wire rack
and slice to serve. **SERVES 8**

TIP
*Monkey bread is best served freshly
baked and warm, when it's golden,
sticky and caramelised. It's the
perfect cosy treat to go with coffee.*

chocolate and hazelnut scrolls

plain (all-purpose) flour, for dusting
1 x quantity sweet dough (see *basic recipe*)
200g dark chocolate, finely chopped
½ cup (70g) roasted hazelnuts, finely chopped
milk, for brushing

Lightly grease 10 x ¾-cup-capacity (180ml) Texas muffin
tins and set aside.

Turn the dough out onto a lightly floured surface. Roll
into a 30cm x 40cm rectangle. With the long edge facing
towards you, sprinkle the dough with the chocolate and
hazelnut and roll to make 1 long log. Using a knife lightly
dusted in flour[+], slice into 4cm-thick pieces and place,
cut-side up, into the prepared tins. Cover with plastic
wrap and set aside in a warm place for 1 hour or until
doubled in size.

Preheat oven to 180°C (350°F). Brush the scrolls with
milk and bake for 18–20 minutes or until golden brown.
Allow to cool in the tins for 5 minutes before turning out
onto wire racks to cool slightly. Serve warm. **MAKES 10**

NOTE
*+ A knife dusted in flour will help you
to cut the scrolls neatly and cleanly.*

rustic berry and almond galettes

plain (all-purpose) flour, for dusting
1 x quantity sweet dough (see *basic recipe*)
½ cup (60g) almond meal (ground almonds)
¼ cup (55g) caster (superfine) sugar
40g unsalted butter, melted
250g strawberries, trimmed and halved
100g raspberries
double (thick) cream* and vanilla bean paste, to serve

Preheat oven to 150°C (300°F). Turn the dough out onto a
lightly floured surface. Divide the dough in half and roll
each piece out between sheets of non-stick baking paper
into a 20cm round. Place each round on a baking tray and
remove the top sheets of baking paper. Place the almond
meal, sugar and butter in a medium bowl and mix to
combine. Divide the almond mixture between the dough
rounds and top with the berries. Bake for 25–30 minutes
or until golden. Top with cream and vanilla to serve. **MAKES 2**

rustic berry and almond galettes

GLOSSARY AND INDEX

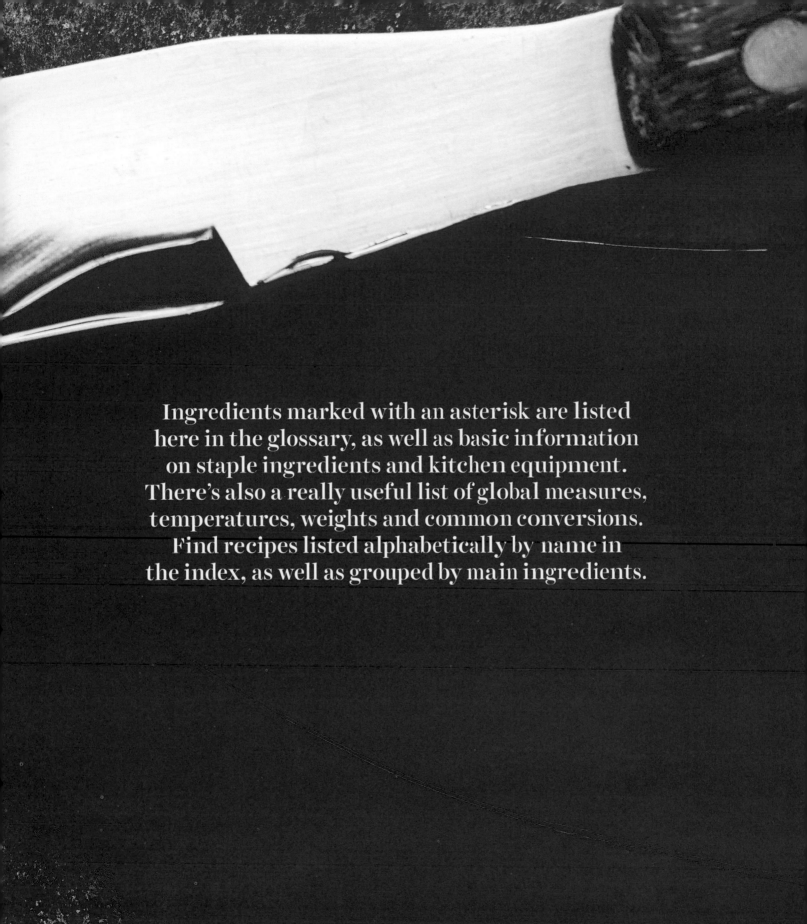

Ingredients marked with an asterisk are listed
here in the glossary, as well as basic information
on staple ingredients and kitchen equipment.
There's also a really useful list of global measures,
temperatures, weights and common conversions.
Find recipes listed alphabetically by name in
the index, as well as grouped by main ingredients.

MARKED INGREDIENTS

ancho chillies
Ancho chillies are a sweet and smoky Mexican poblano pepper. They're available dried from spice shops, some greengrocers and online. They have a smouldering, smoky flavour that's great in slow-cooked dishes.

blue swimmer crab
A common edible crab named for its vibrant blue-coloured shell. Available green (uncooked) and cooked from fish shops and markets. Ask your fishmonger to cut and clean the crab for you if necessary, and eat on the same day of purchase.

bok choy
A mild-flavoured green vegetable, also known as Chinese chard or Chinese white cabbage. It's best lightly steamed, blanched or pan-fried and goes well with Asian dishes, rice and stir-fries. Baby bok choy can be cooked whole, but it's best to trim the white stalks and separate the leaves from the larger variety.

brioche slider buns
Soft and light with a glossy exterior, these small French-style brioche rolls are perfect for making mini burgers or sliders filled with brisket or pulled pork. Find brioche buns at most bakeries, specialty and Italian grocers and some supermarkets.

brisket
A cut of beef from the front underside, or breast section, of the animal. Brisket calls for long slow cooking, roasting, barbecuing or braising and is often paired with smoky, Southern-style flavours. Available from butchers and most supermarkets.

broccolini (tenderstem)
Also known as tenderstem broccoli, broccolini is a cross between gai lan (Chinese broccoli) and broccoli. This green vegetable has long, thin stems and small florets with a slightly sweet flavour. Sold in bunches, it can be substituted for regular heads of broccoli.

butter beans
Large, plump white beans also known as lima beans. They go well in soups, stews and salads. Available from delicatessens and supermarkets either canned or in dried form. Dried beans need to be soaked in water before cooking, and canned simply rinsed and drained.

buttermilk
Once a by-product of the butter churning process, commercial buttermilk is created by adding a bacteria to skimmed milk. Its acidity and tangy creaminess is often harnessed to make fluffy pancakes, moist cakes, light scones and rich dressings. It's sold in cartons at supermarkets.

cavolo nero (tuscan kale)
Translated to mean 'black cabbage', this robust leafy vegetable is named so for its inky green leaves. Similar to silverbeet and equally rich in nutrients, it's in season in winter and perfect for adding to hearty soups, stews and pastas. Trim before use.

char siu sauce
Commonly used in Cantonese cuisine to flavour pork, char siu contains sugar or honey, Chinese five-spice, soy sauce, red food colouring and sherry. Available from supermarkets and Asian grocers.

cheese
bocconcini
Small, bite-sized balls of the fresh mild Italian cheese, mozzarella. Sold in tubs in a lightly salted brine, bocconcini spoils easily so is best consumed within 2 or 3 days.

buffalo mozzarella
A much-loved variety of fresh Italian mozzarella, made from water buffalo's milk and/or cow's milk. Creamy and salty, it's sold in rounds at grocers and delicatessens and is often torn and scattered over caprese salads or pizza.

burrata
An Italian stretched-curd cheese made from mozzarella, burrata has a creamy, milky centre. It's best served simply, with something like a tomato or fig salad. It's available from delicatessens, specialty cheese stores and Italian grocery stores.

goat's cheese
Goat's milk has a tart flavour, so the cheese made from it, also called chèvre, has a sharp, slightly acidic taste. Immature goat's cheese is mild and creamy and is often labelled goat's curd, which is smooth and spreadable. Mature goat's cheese is available in both hard and soft varieties.

gruyere
A firm cow's milk cheese with a smooth ivory interior and a natural brushed rind. Popular in Switzerland as a table cheese and cooked into fondues, gratins and quiches. It makes a fabulous melting cheese, especially in toasted sandwiches.

manchego
Firm ivory-yellow cheese of Spanish origin made from sheep's milk. It has a subtle, buttery flavour.

mascarpone
A fresh Italian triple-cream curd-style cheese, mascarpone has a smooth consistency, similar to thick (double) cream. Available in tubs from specialty food stores, delicatessens and some supermarkets, it's used in sauces and desserts such as tiramisu, as well as in icings and frostings for its luscious creaminess and subtle tang.

pecorino
A popular hard Italian cheese made from sheep's milk, pecorino has a sharp flavour similar to that of parmesan cheese. Available at delicatessens, cheese shops and most supermarkets. If unavailable, substitute with parmesan.

provolone
A firm buttery, mild-flavoured Italian cheese, similar to mozzarella. Provolone piccante is sharper in flavour, whereas provolone dolce is sweeter and creamier.

chervil
A herb that's related to parsley, with soft lacy leaves and a more delicate flavour. It has a slight aniseed aroma. Chervil is often used in French cuisine, and due to its subtlety, works best in salads or soups.

chinese cooking wine (shaoxing)
Similar to dry sherry, Shaoxing or Chinese cooking wine is a blend of glutinous rice, millet, a special yeast and the local spring waters of Shaoxing in northern China, where it is traditionally made. Used in myriad sauces and dressings, it's available from the Asian section of supermarkets and at Asian grocery stores.

chinese five-spice powder
A fragrant ground blend of cinnamon, Sichuan pepper, star anise, cloves and fennel seeds, five spice is a popular seasoning for duck and pork. It also goes well with chicken, lamb and beef. It's an essential ingredient in slow-braised Chinese dishes. Available at Asian food stores, spice shops and supermarkets.

chinese pancakes
Also known as Mandarin pancakes, these soft thin rounds are commonly used to enclose crispy Peking duck. Buy them ready made from Asian grocers or find them in kits paired with Asian sauces at most supermarkets.

chorizo
Firm, spicy, coarse-textured Spanish pork sausage seasoned with pepper, paprika and chillies. Available fresh and dried from butchers and delicatessens.

coconut
flakes
Coconut flakes have a large shape and chewier texture than the desiccated variety and are often used for decorating and in cereals and baking.

milk
A milky, sweet liquid made by soaking grated fresh coconut flesh or desiccated coconut in warm water and squeezing it through muslin or cheesecloth to extract the liquid. Available in cans or freeze-dried from supermarkets, coconut milk should not be confused with coconut juice, which is a clear liquid found inside young coconuts.

shredded
Coarser than desiccated coconut, shredded coconut is perfect for baking into slices, or for making condiments to go with curries.

cream
The fat content determines the names of the different types of cream and their uses.

double (thick)
Often called heavy cream, this has a butter fat content of 40–50 per cent. It is usually served on the side of warm puddings or rich cakes.

single (pouring)
Has a butter fat content of 20–30 per cent. It is the type of cream most commonly used for making ice-cream, panna cotta and custard. It can be whipped to a light and airy consistency. Often called pure or whipping cream.

thickened
This is a single (pouring) cream that has had a vegetable gum added to stabilise it. The gum makes the cream a little thicker and easier to whip.

daikon
A large white variety of Asian radish, daikon can be pickled, shredded raw into salads, or sliced and cooked in dishes such as stir-fries. It's commonly found in Chinese and Japanese cuisines, but its mild flavour and crisp texture make it versatile.

dutch cocoa
Dutch or Dutch-processed cocoa is regular cocoa that has been alkalised to remove some of its naturally occurring bitterness and acidity. This yields a darker-coloured powder with a rich, mellow flavour. Available in the baking aisle of supermarkets.

fish sauce
An amber-coloured liquid drained from salted, fermented fish and used to add flavour to Thai and Vietnamese dishes such as curries and in dressings for salads. There are different grades available.

gai lan (chinese broccoli)
Also known as Chinese broccoli or Chinese kale, gai lan is a leafy vegetable with dark green leaves, tiny white or yellow flowers and stout stems. It can be steamed or blanched and served with oyster sauce as a simple side or added to soups, stir-fries and braises towards the end of the cooking time. Sold in bunches at greengrocers and supermarkets.

galangal
A rhizome with cream or pink skin and a knobbly exterior, galangal is related (and looks similar) to ginger but has a milder flavour. It's used widely in Thai and Malaysian cuisine, especially in soups and pastes. You can find it at greengrocers.

ginger nut biscuits

A popular, commercially-made sweet biscuit flavoured with ground ginger and spices. Sometimes used crushed or ground in baking to make biscuit bases for slices and cheesecakes. Similar but different to ginger snap biscuits – ginger nuts are very hard in texture. Sold in packs at supermarkets.

gow gee wrappers

Chinese in origin, these round, thin sheets of dough are available fresh or frozen. They can be steamed or fried. Fill them with meat and vegetables to make dumplings, or use as a crunchy base for nibbles.

green mango

Unripe or green mangoes have a sour flavour and are used in Southeast Asian cuisine in chutneys and salads. They're particularly popular in Thai-style salads.

green papaya

Like green mango, unripe papaya has a starring role in Thai salads, where it is shredded and served with a dressing of lime, fish sauce, palm sugar and chilli. This popular dish is called som tam.

hoisin sauce

A thick, sweet Chinese sauce made from fermented soybeans, sugar, salt and red rice. Used as a dipping sauce or marinade and as the sauce for Peking duck, hoisin is available from Asian grocery stores and most supermarkets.

jalapeños

Dark green plump Mexican chillies, known for their medium heat and fresh, bitey flavour. Buy jalapeños sliced in jars, pickled, or fresh. Often served with tacos and other popular Mexican cuisine, much of their heat is held in the seeds and membranes, which can be removed for a milder intensity.

japanese mayonnaise

Also called Kewpie mayonnaise, this Japanese blend is sold in squeezable bottles at Asian grocers and most supermarkets. It's popular for its umami flavour and slight sweetness. It's used in sushi, as a substitute for regular mayonnaise and as a dipping sauce.

kaffir lime leaves

Fragrant leaves with a distinctive double-leaf structure, used crushed or shredded in Thai dishes. Available fresh or dried from Asian food stores.

kimchi

A pungent Korean cabbage condiment, loved for its sour fermented flavour. Available ready made from Asian grocery stores, it's becoming increasingly popular for lending its spicy flavour kick to all kinds of dishes, Korean and otherwise.

lemongrass

A tall lemon-scented grass used in Asian cooking, particularly in Thai dishes. Peel away the outer leaves and chop the tender white root-end finely, or add it in large pieces during cooking and remove before serving. If adding in bigger pieces, bruise them with the back of a large knife.

lime pickle

A traditional Indian condiment made from lime, spices and chillies. You can find ready-made lime pickle in jars at the supermarket – it's usually in the aisle with the curry pastes.

marinated artichoke hearts

The soft, flavourful centres of globe artichokes that have been marinated in oil or a bitey pickling vinegar. Often served as part of an antipasto plate, sprinkled onto pizzas or tossed through pasta, buy this pantry staple in jars or by weight from delicatessens, Italian grocers or supermarkets.

marjoram

A delicately flavoured herb, related to mint and very similar in flavour to oregano.

mirin (japanese rice wine)

A pale yellow Japanese cooking wine made from glutinous rice and alcohol. Sweet mirin is flavoured with corn syrup.

miso paste

A traditional Japanese ingredient produced by fermenting rice, barley or soy beans to a paste. It is used for sauces and spreads, pickling vegetables, and is often mixed with dashi stock to serve as miso soup. Often labelled simply 'miso', white, yellow and red varieties are available, their flavour increasing in intensity with their colour. Find in supermarkets and Asian grocers.

oyster sauce

A rich, dark brown Asian sauce, often used in stir-fries. Made from oysters, soy sauce and varying other ingredients, it gives a full salty-sweet flavour to dishes. It's sold in the Asian aisle of supermarkets.

palm sugar

Produced by tapping the sap of palm trees, palm sugar is allowed to crystallise, then is sold in cubes or round blocks, which you can shave and add to curries, dressings and Asian desserts. Available from supermarkets and Asian food stores.

pancetta

A cured and rolled Italian-style meat that is like prosciutto but less salty and with a softer texture. It's sold in flat pieces or chunks, or is thinly sliced into rounds. It can be eaten both uncooked and cooked.

pappadums

Microwave (or fry) pappadums as the label instructs. You can also buy ready-puffed mini pappadums in foil bags, similar to crisps, which are useful to have on-hand in the pantry. Sold in supermarkets.

paprika

smoked

Unlike Hungarian paprika, the Spanish style known as pimentón is deep and smoky in flavour. It is made from smoked, ground pimento peppers and comes in varying intensities from sweet and mild (dulce), bittersweet medium hot (agridulce) and hot (picante).

sweet

Made from dried, ground red capsicums (peppers), this earthy coloured powder is used as a spice, seasoning and garnish.

pastry

Make your own or use one of the many store-bought varieties, including shortcrust and filo, which are sold frozen in blocks or ready-rolled into pastry sheets. Defrost in the fridge before use.

puff and butter puff

This pastry is quite difficult to make, so many cooks opt to use store-bought puff pastry. It can be bought in blocks from patisseries, or is sold in both block and sheet forms in supermarkets. Butter puff pastry is very light and flaky, perfect for sweet pies and tarts. Often labeled 'all butter puff', good-quality sheets are usually thicker. If you can only buy thin sheets of butter puff, don't be afraid to stack 2 thawed sheets together.

pea eggplants

These small Thai eggplants, roughly the size of peas, are often used in Thai soups or curries for their interesting bitter flavour. Sold on their stems, like a sprig of green berries, find pea eggplants at specialty greengrocers or Asian grocers.

pickled ginger

Also known as gari, this Japanese condiment is made from young ginger that's been pickled in sugar and vinegar. It's commonly served with sushi.

ponzu sauce

A tangy Japanese dressing made with citrus or rice wine vinegar, soy sauce, mirin, kombu and dried bonito flakes. Available in supermarkets, use it in marinades or as a dipping sauce.

prosciutto

Italian ham that's been salted and dried for up to two years. The paper-thin slices are eaten raw or used to lend their distinctive flavour to braises and other cooked dishes.

rose petals, edible dried

Pesticide-free, organic rose petals are sold dried in packs at cake decorating stores, specialty food shops and online. Ensure the packaging states they're edible. They can be used on all kinds of sweet treats.

rosewater

An essence distilled from rose petals, rosewater is one of the cornerstone flavours of Indian, Middle-Eastern and Turkish tables. It's usually used in sweets and is the distinctive flavour in Turkish delight (lokum).

sanding sugar

A coarse-grained sugar used for decorating cakes, cupcakes and cookies. It holds its shape when baked for extra crunch and texture. It's also available in colours. Sold at cake decorating stores and online.

shrimp paste

Made from small fermented shrimp and often called blachan, this paste is used in stir-fries and curries to give a pungent depth of flavour. It's available from Asian supermarkets and grocery stores.

sichuan peppercorns

Not a pepper, but dried berries with a spicy, tongue-tingling effect, sold whole. Toast in a hot, dry frying pan until fragrant before crushing or grinding. Popular in the coating for salt and pepper squid.

squid hoods

Squid, often called and very similar to calamari, is best cooked for short amounts of time on the day of purchase, to ensure freshness and tenderness. The cleaned hoods, or tubes (the body of the squid), are sold at fish shops and supermarket delis.

streaky bacon

Also known as American-style bacon or belly bacon, streaky bacon is from the back end of the pork loin. Cured and smoked, it's often sold in thin strips or slices and can now be found in most supermarkets and at specialty grocers.

tabasco green pepper sauce

Milder than the original hot sauce, Tabasco's Green Pepper Sauce is made from jalapeños. You can find the Tabasco range in most supermarkets, or substitute it with another jalapeño hot sauce.

tahini

A thick paste made from ground sesame seeds. Used in Middle-Eastern cooking, it's available in jars and cans from supermarkets and health food shops. It is used to make the popular dip hummus.

water chestnuts

Popular in Asian stir-fries, water chestnuts are the crunchy white tuber of a water-plant native to Southeast Asia. They're available canned in the supermarket, or buy them fresh from Asian grocers and peel before use.

whole-wheat couscous

Couscous is a traditional North-African staple, commonly served with spices, meats and tagines. Whole-wheat couscous, made from whole durum wheat, is less refined than regular couscous and thus more nutritious. Find it in the health food section of your supermarket. For more flavour, use stock rather than water to soak the couscous.

BASICS

aioli
A garlic-flavoured mayonnaise that's a popular condiment in Spanish and French cuisines. You can buy it in jars, in varying degrees of quality, at most supermarkets and delicatessens.

almond meal (ground almonds)
Often referred to as ground almonds, almond meal is available from most supermarkets and grocers. Make your own by processing whole skinned almonds to a fine meal in a food processor or blender (125g almonds will give 1 cup almond meal). To remove the skins from almonds, soak in boiling water, then, using your fingers, slide the skins off.

baking powder
A raising agent used in baking, consisting of bicarbonate of soda and/or cream of tartar. Most are gluten free (check the labels). Baking powder that's kept beyond its use-by date can lose effectiveness. For a makeshift self-raising (self-rising) flour, add 2 teaspoons of baking powder to each 1 cup (150g) of plain (all-purpose) flour and sift repeatedly to combine.

bay leaves
These aromatic leaves of the bay tree are available both fresh from some greengrocers and dried from the spice section of supermarkets. Add to soups, stews and stocks for a savoury depth of flavour. Remove before serving.

bicarbonate of (baking) soda
Also known as baking soda, bicarbonate of soda (sodium bicarbonate) is an alkaline powder used to help leaven baked goods and neutralise acids. It's also often hailed as having multiple uses around the home, notably as an effective cleaner.

blanching
A cooking method used to slightly soften the texture, heighten the colour and enhance the flavour of foods, namely vegetables. Plunge the ingredient briefly into boiling unsalted water, then remove and refresh under cold water. Drain well.

butter
Unless stated otherwise in a recipe, butter should be at room temperature for cooking. It should not be half-melted or too soft to handle. We use unsalted butter in most recipes.

cabbage
chinese (wombok)
Also known as wombok or Napa cabbage, Chinese cabbage is elongated in shape with ribbed green-yellow leaves. It's often used in noodle salads and to make kimchi. Find it at Asian grocers and greengrocers.

white
White or pale green with tightly bound, waxy leaves, these common cabbages are sold whole or halved in supermarkets and are perfect for use in slaws and sides. Choose heads that are firm and unblemished with crispy leaves.

capers
The small green flower buds of the caper bush. Available packed either in brine or salt, capers lend their signature salty-sour intensity to sauces, seafood, pastas and more. Before using, rinse thoroughly, drain and pat dry.

caramelised onion relish
Sliced onion that's been cooked slowly to release all its sugars. Made even more intense in flavour by the addition of brown sugar and balsamic vinegar. It's sold in most supermarkets as a condiment and is handy to have in the pantry as a shortcut to flavour for pizzas, tarts and grilled meats.

cheese
blue
The distinctive blue veins and strong flavour of blue cheeses are achieved by adding a cultured mould. Most have a soft-yet-crumbly texture and acidic taste, which becomes rounded and more mellow with age. Blue cheeses team particularly well with sweet flavours – they're often paired on cheese boards and in salads with quince paste, pear, honey or figs.

cream
A fresh, salted, spreadable cheese sold in tubs or foil-wrapped blocks. Used both as a spread for sandwiches and bagels or as the base for a cream cheese frosting.

haloumi
A firm white Cypriot cheese made from sheep's milk. It has a stringy texture and is usually sold in brine. Slice and pan-fry until golden and heated through for a creamy, salty addition to salads. Available from delicatessens, grocers and supermarkets.

marinated feta
Pieces of the creamy, sharp-tasting Greek-style cheese that have been marinated in oil, often with a mix of herbs, garlic and peppercorns. Find jars and tubs of marinated feta at supermarkets, gourmet food stores and delicatessens.

mozzarella
Italian in origin, mozzarella is the mild, fresh white cheese of pizza, lasagne and tomato salads. It's made by cutting and spinning (or stringing) the curd to achieve a smooth, elastic consistency. Types of mozzarella include bocconcini, buffalo mozzarella and burrata. Buy fresh mozzarella from supermarkets, grocers and delicatessens. Supermarkets also sell a packaged, grated mozzarella, which is different to the fresh variety – it's usually pale yellow in colour and drier in texture.

parmesan

Italy's favourite hard, granular cheese is made from cow's milk. Parmigiano Reggiano is the best variety, made under strict guidelines in the Emilia-Romagna region and aged for an average of two years. Grana Padano mainly comes from Lombardy and is aged for around 15 months.

ricotta

A creamy, finely grained white cheese. Ricotta means 'recooked' in Italian, a reference to the way the cheese is produced by heating the whey leftover from making other cheeses. Fresh full-cream and low-fat ricotta is available at the deli counter of supermarkets. The fresh full-cream variety is best for making gnocchi, cheesecakes and pancakes, and shouldn't be substituted for the smoother variety that's pre-packaged in tubs.

chickpeas (garbanzo beans)

Legumes with a nutty flavour, used often in Middle-Eastern, Meditteranean and Indian cooking. If not ground into besan flour, they're used whole in soups and stews or blended into hummus. Dried chickpeas must be soaked before cooking, canned chickpeas just rinsed and drained.

chilli bean paste

Made from salted black beans mixed with chilli, garlic and star anise, this is a pungent sauce of the Asian kitchen. It adds a great depth of flavour and is available from Asian supermarkets and grocery stores.

chillies

There are more than 200 different types of chilli in the world. By general rule of thumb, long red and green chillies are milder, fruitier and sweeter, while small chillies (sometimes called birdseye) are much hotter. Taking this into account, we specify either large or small chillies in our recipes. Remove the membrane and seeds for a milder result.

chocolate

dark

Rich and semi-sweet, regular dark chocolate usually contains 45–55% cocoa solids. It's sold in blocks and is ideal for use in baking. Dark chocolate that has 70% cocoa solids is usually labelled as such, and has a more bitter, intense flavour with a slightly powdery texture.

milk

Sweet, creamy and smooth, with a lighter colour than dark chocolate, milk chocolate is the most popular for eating. Sold in blocks, it usually contains around 25% cocoa solids.

coriander (cilantro)

This aromatic green herb is also called cilantro. The delicate leaves have a signature flavour and, sometimes along with the finely chopped roots and stems, are commonly used in Asian and Mexican cooking.

coriander seeds

These dried seeds of the coriander plant are an Indian staple. They're sold ground or whole and are one of the base ingredients in curry. They're different to (and cannot be substituted for) the fresh leaves.

cos (romaine) lettuce

The star of Caesar salads, this elongated crispy lettuce has dark green outer leaves and a pale green-yellow centre (heart). Baby cos, or gem lettuce, has also become readily available for its sweet crisp flavour.

cumin seeds

This ancient spice, from a plant of the parsley family, is common in Middle-Eastern and Indian cooking. The small long brown seeds are peppery and aromatic with distinct flavour, particularly when toasted. Buy cumin seeds, whole or ground, from the spice section of supermarkets.

curry leaves

Sold fresh or dried, curry leaves can be used in much the same way as bay leaves or kaffir lime leaves. They impart a fragrance, aroma and savoury flavour to a dish but are removed before serving. With their slightly spicy, aromatic citrus notes, curry leaves are perfect stirred into curries and chutneys.

dill

A flavourful herb with feathery fronds, dill is used mostly fresh in salads or as a garnish. Both the fronds and seeds are used in the pickling of cucumbers and give dill pickles their signature flavour. If cooking with dill, add it in the last moments as heat can reduce its intensity.

dulce de leche

This is a thick South-American milk caramel made by slowly heating and thickening sweetened milk. You can buy it in jars and use it to fill biscuits, pies, tarts and more. You can also make your own cheat's version by baking sweetened condensed milk.

edamame

The Japanese name for baby soy beans, edamame are usually sold frozen in the pod. Small and green with a mild flavour and unique texture, they can be quickly steamed or blanched and served simply as a snack with a little salt as they are in many Japanese restaurants, or they can be podded and tossed through salads and sides. Find them in the freezer section at major supermarkets and Asian grocers.

eggs

The standard egg size used in this book is 60g. It is important to use the right sized eggs for a recipe, as this will affect the outcome of baked goods. The correct volume is especially important when using eggwhites to make meringues. You should use eggs at room temperature for baking.

eschalots (French shallots)

A member of the onion family, eschalots are smaller and have a milder flavour than brown, red or white onions. Used often in Europe, they look like small elongated brown onions with purple-grey tinged skins.

fennel

Sometimes called finocchio, it's the Florence fennel plant that's known for its bulb and fronds. The bulb can be eaten fresh, shaved into salads, or cooked, which brings out its sweetness. Use the aniseed-flavoured fronds as a herb.

seeds

The green seeds of the common fennel plant impart a warm anise note to breads and chutneys as well as fish, meat and vegetable dishes. Toast and/or grind them for maximum flavour.

flour

cornflour (cornstarch)

When made from ground corn or maize, cornflour is gluten free. It's quite often blended with water or stock to be used as a thickening agent. Not to be confused with cornflour in the United States, which is finely ground corn meal.

plain (all-purpose)

Ground from the endosperm of wheat, plain white flour contains no raising agent.

rice

A fine flour made from white rice. Used as a thickening agent in baking and to coat tofu or chicken in Asian dishes for a crispy finish.

self-raising (self-rising)

Ground from the endosperm of wheat, self-raising flour contains raising agents including sodium carbonates and calcium phosphates. To make it using plain flour, add 2 teaspoons of baking powder to every 1 cup (150g) of flour.

spelt

Milled from the ancient cereal grain, spelt flour can, in some cases, be used in place of regular wheat flour – it boasts more nutrients and is better tolerated by some. It lends baked goods a nutty flavour and caramel colour. Sold at health food stores and some supermarkets, white spelt flour is easier to bake with, while wholemeal retains more of the grain's goodness.

green onions (scallions)

Both the white and green part of these long mild onions are used in salads, as a garnish and in Asian cooking. Sold in bunches, they give a fresh bite to dishes.

harissa

A North-African condiment, harissa is a hot red paste made from chilli, garlic and spices including coriander, caraway and cumin. It can also contain tomato. Available in jars and tubes from supermarkets and specialty food stores, harissa enlivens tagines and couscous dishes and can be added to dressings and sauces for an instant flavour kick.

horseradish

A pungent root vegetable that releases mustard oil when cut or grated. It oxidises quickly, so use immediately after cutting or cover with water or vinegar. Fresh horseradish is lovely grated over beef or roast pork; find it at greengrocers. You can also buy the grated product or horseradish cream in jars from the supermarket.

hummus

A popular dip of the Middle East, made by blending chickpeas (garbanzo beans) with tahini, garlic and lemon juice. With its pleasant nutty flavour and slightly grainy texture, hummus is served alongside all manner of grilled meats, flatbreads and salads. Available in tubs from supermarkets.

maple syrup

A sweetener made from the sap of the maple tree. Be sure to use pure maple syrup rather than imitation or maple-flavoured pancake syrup.

micro herbs

The baby version of fresh herbs, these tiny edible leaves have a great intensity of flavour despite their size. They make a beautiful garnish and addition to salads. Available in small pots and in a loose mix at farmers' markets and greengrocers.

mushrooms

button

This tender little mushroom, tightly closed around its stalk, is the young form of the commercial field mushroom. White and mildly flavoured, it can be used raw in salads but is tastier when cooked in stews, stir-fries and pasta sauces.

enoki

This Japanese mushroom has a long white stalk with a small bulb at the end. It goes well in soups, salads and stir-fries and should only be added at the very end of the cooking time.

oyster

This shell-shaped mushroom, sometimes called abalone, has a delicate flavour and tender bite. Colours range from pearly white to apricot-pink. Tear, rather than cut, and cook gently, whether simmering in soups, pan-frying or grilling. Be aware that when eaten raw, they can, at times, trigger an allergic reaction.

pine

Also known as saffron milk caps, these large-capped mushrooms have a pretty orange hue and are found growing around pine trees. They have a nutty flavour and firm texture and keep their shape when cooked. You can find them at some greengrocers and farmer's markets.

porcini
Available fresh in Europe and the UK and sold dried elsewhere, including Australia and the US. They have an almost meaty texture and earthy taste. Soak dried porcini mushrooms before using, and use the soaking liquid as a stock if desired. Frozen porcinis are becoming readily available. Like the dried variety, they're available from specialty food stores.

portobello
This large flat mushroom is closely related to the white field mushroom but has a nutty, rich flavour and brown flaky skin. A mature version of the Swiss brown, its meaty texture makes it suitable for robust cooking styles.

shiitake
Tan to dark brown with a meaty texture and earthy taste akin to wild mushrooms. Its dried form, found in Asian food stores, gives the most intense flavour.

swiss brown
A button version of the portobello and a more flavoursome substitute for the common white mushroom. Use Swiss browns in pasta sauces, risottos or braises.

mustard

dijon
Also called French mustard, this creamy, mild-flavoured condiment originated in France. Often used to make vinaigrette.

hot english
Pungent and yellow in colour with an intense heat, pair English mustard with ham or roast beef.

seeds
Of the mustard plant. Available in varying colours from white and yellow to brown and black (the pungency intensifies with the colour). Used to make mustards and condiments, as well as to flavour curries.

noodles

Used in Asian stir-fries, soups and salads, keep a supply of dried noodles in the pantry for last-minute meals. Fresh noodles will keep in the fridge for up to 1 week. Rice, egg and wheat varieties are available from supermarkets.

nori

Thin sheets of dried, vitamin-packed seaweed used in Japanese-style dishes and to wrap sushi. Available in packets from supermarkets and Asian food stores.

oil

chilli
Vegetable oil infused with hot chillies, often served with dumplings and soups. Find chilli oil at Asian grocers.

olive
Graded according to its flavour, aroma and acidity. Extra virgin is the highest quality; it contains no more than 1% acid. Virgin is the next best; it contains 1.5% or less acid. Bottles labelled simply 'olive oil' contain a blend of refined and unrefined virgin olive oil. 'Light' olive oil is the least pure in quality and shouldn't be confused with light-flavoured extra virgin olive oil.

peanut
Made from ground peanuts, this oil is most often used in Asian cooking for its high smoke point, or ability to heat without burning.

sesame
Pressed from sesame seeds, sesame oil is used in Asian cuisine more as a nutty, full-flavoured seasoning than a cooking medium.

vegetable
Oils sourced from plants or seeds, with very mild, unobtrusive flavours. Often called for in baking recipes, such as muffins or loaf cakes, for this reason.

olives

black
Black olives are more mature and less salty than the green variety. Choose firm olives with good colour and a fruity taste.

green
Green olives are picked when unripe, making them denser in texture than black olives.

kalamata
Greek in origin, fleshy Kalamata olives have an intense flavour, which makes them the ideal choice for Greek salads and for use in tapenades. Dark brown and glossy, they are sometimes sold split.

sicilian
A variety of green olive, common in Sicilian cuisine, that are large and plump in size, bright in colour and fruity in flavour.

tapenade
A paste made by blending olives, capers, garlic and anchovies with oil. Served as a dip with crackers, or spread on bruschetta and pizzas, it makes a good marinade and partner for cold meats or cheeses.

pistachio

A delicately flavoured green nut inside a hard outer shell, pistachios are available salted or unsalted. They're commonly used in Middle-Eastern cuisine as well as in salads and sweets, such as baklava.

preserved lemon

Preserved lemons are lemons rubbed with salt, packed in jars, covered with lemon juice and left for about four weeks. They're often flavoured with cloves, cinnamon or chilli. Discard the flesh, rinse and chop the rind for use in cooking. They're popular in Moroccan cuisine, where they're added to tagines, and they also make a zesty addition to salad dressing. Available from delicatessens and speciality food stores.

quinoa

Not a grain but actually a seed, originating in South America. Packed with protein, it has a chewy texture, nutty flavour and is fluffy when cooked. The most common variety is white, which is mild in taste, while the red variety has a stronger flavour and crunch. Use as you would couscous or rice.

ras el hanout

A spice mix literally translating to 'top of the shop', ras el hanout can contain more than 20 different spices, most commonly cinnamon, cardamom, cloves, coriander, chilli, paprika and turmeric. Find it at spice shops and most greengrocers.

rice

arborio

Rice with a short, plump-looking grain that cooks to a soft texture, while retaining a firm interior. It has surface starch that creates a creamy texture in risottos when cooked to al dente. Available at specialty food stores and most supermarkets.

basmati

A fragrant long-grained rice with a slightly nutty flavour. Non-sticky when cooked, it's commonly used in Indian and Middle-Eastern cooking.

brown

Retains the bran of the rice grain (which is removed from white rice) making it high in fibre and more nutritious. Brown rice takes longer to cook than white rice, and has a signature chewiness.

jasmine

Also called Thai fragrant rice, jasmine is an aromatic long-grained white rice used often in Southeast-Asian cooking.

sushi

A plump, short-grained white rice used for making sushi. It can also be served as a side to Japanese meat dishes.

sage

A Mediterranean herb with a distinct, fragrant flavour. Commonly used in Italian cooking and often crisped in a pan with butter or oil.

sesame seeds

These small glossy seeds have a creamy, nutty flavour and can be used in savoury and sweet cooking. White sesame seeds are the most common variety, but black, or unhulled, seeds are popular for coatings in Asian cooking as well as some Asian desserts. Sesame oil is made by extracting the oil from the seeds.

shiso leaves

Sometimes called perilla, this herb comes in both green and purple-leafed varieties. It has a slight peppery flavour and is often used to to wrap ingredients. The micro variety makes a pretty garnish. Find it at some greengrocers and Asian markets.

silverbeet (swiss chard)

A vegetable with large, crinkly, glossy dark green leaves and prominent white, red or yellow stalks. Rich in nutrients, it can be used in salads, soups, pies and steamed as a green side. Not to be confused with spinach which has a smaller and more delicate leaf, silverbeet is best trimmed and washed before use.

spring onions

Often confused with, and with a more pronounced bulb than green onions (scallions), the spring or salad onion is great in salads, soups and stir-fries. It can also be slow-cooked until caramelised and served whole or pureed.

star anise

A small brown seed cluster that is shaped like a star. It has a strong aniseed flavour and can be used whole or ground in sweet and savoury dishes. It works well in master stocks or braises.

sugar

Extracted as crystals from the juice of the sugarcane plant or beet, sugar is a sweetener, flavour enhancer, bulking agent and preservative.

brown

Processed with molasses, brown sugar comes in differing shades of brown, according to the quantity of molasses added (which varies between countries). This, in turn, affects the taste of the sugar and thus the result of baked treats and desserts made with it – from light caramel flavours to rich, deep toffee notes.

caster (superfine)

The most commonly called for sugar in this book, caster sugar gives baked products a light texture and delicate crumb, thanks to its fine grain. Important in many cakes as well as airy desserts such as meringues. It dissolves easily.

demerara

This sugar's large crystals, with their golden colour and mild caramel flavour, give baked goods a pronounced crust, and coffee a distinct flavour. If unavailable, substitute with a mixture of 3 parts white (granulated) sugar to 1 part brown sugar.

icing (confectioner's)

Regular granulated sugar ground to a very fine powder. When mixed with liquid or into butter or cream cheese it creates a sweet glaze or icing, plus it can simply be sifted over cakes or desserts. Unless specified, use pure icing sugar not icing sugar mixture, which contains cornflour (cornstarch) and needs more liquid.

raw caster (superfine)

The honey-caramel flavour of raw sugar in a superfine grain size. Ideal for baking sweet treats like muffins and loaf cakes. Find it in the baking aisle of supermarkets. If unavailable, use regular caster sugar.

white (granulated)

Regular granulated sugar is used in baking when a light texture is not crucial. The crystals are large, so you need to beat, add liquids or heat this sugar to dissolve it.

sumac

Dried berries of a flowering plant are ground to produce an acidic reddish-purple powder, popular in the Middle East. Sumac has a slight lemony flavour and is great sprinkled in salads or on dips.

tarragon

Called the king of herbs by the French and used in many of their classic sauces such as Bérnaise and tartare. It has a slight aniseed flavour.

tomato

heirloom

A non-hybrid cultivar of tomato that's not usually grown on a commercial scale. Large and irregular in appearance with a good, strong flavour, you can find heirloom tomatoes in rich reds, greens and yellows.

paste

This triple-concentrated tomato puree is used as a flavour booster and thickener in soups, sauces and stews. There are salt-reduced varieties available.

puree (passata)

Italian for 'passed', passata is made by removing the skins and seeds from ripe tomatoes and passing the flesh through a sieve to make a thick, rich, tomato puree. Substitute with sugo, which is made from crushed tomatoes so it has a little more texture than passata. Both are available in bottles from supermarkets.

sauce (ketchup)

A sweet, acidic commercially bottled sauce made from tomatoes, vinegar and a sweetener (sugar or fruit). It's a common condiment for sausages and steak.

turmeric

This vibrantly orange root is commonly used in Indian cuisine and is usually ground, dried and sold as a powder to flavour curries. You can find fresh turmeric in Asian grocery stores and some greengrocers.

vanilla

bean paste

This store-bought paste is a convenient way to replace whole vanilla beans and is great in desserts. 1 teaspoon of paste substitutes for 1 vanilla bean. Find it in small jars or tubes in the baking aisle of most supermarkets.

beans

These fragrant cured pods from the vanilla orchid are used whole, often split with the tiny seeds inside scraped into the mixture, to infuse flavour into custard and cream-based recipes. They offer a rich and rounded vanilla flavour.

extract

Syrup-like and readily available from the baking aisle of supermarkets, choose a good-quality vanilla extract, not an essence or imitation flavour.

vinegar

apple cider

Made from apple must, cider vinegar has a golden amber hue and a sour appley flavour. Use it in dressings, marinades and chutneys.

balsamic

Originally from Modena in Italy, there are many varieties on the market, ranging in quality and flavour. Aged balsamics are generally preferable. Also available in a milder white version, made with white, as opposed to red, wine. It's milder in flavour and is not as sweet as its dark cousin. Use white balsamic in dishes where the colour is important.

chinese black

A rich, smoky dark vinegar. Served as a dipping sauce with dumplings or used as a seasoning. Find it at Asian grocers and most supermarkets.

malt

Produced from ale made from malted barley, this vinegar is typically light brown in colour. Used in pickles and chutneys, some also feel it's the natural partner for fish and chips.

rice wine

Made from fermenting rice or rice wine, rice vinegar is milder and sweeter than vinegars made by oxidising distilled alcohol or wine made from grapes. Rice wine vinegar is available in white (colourless to pale yellow), black and red varieties from Asian food stores and some supermarkets.

white

A strong, everyday vinegar made from distilled grain alcohol.

wine

Both red and white wine can be distilled into vinegar for use in dressings, glazes, sauces and preserved condiments such as pickles. This is the vinegar to use in the classic French dressing, vinaigrette.

yeast, dry

Sometimes called active dry yeast, this granular raising agent is primarily used to make dough for breads, pizzas and sweet baked treats. Buy it in sachets from the supermarket.

yoghurt

natural Greek-style (thick)

The recipes in this book call for natural, unsweetened, full-fat Greek-style (thick) yoghurt. Pairing well with both sweet and savoury dishes, buy it in tubs from the chilled section of the supermarket, checking the label for any added sugars.

EQUIPMENT

bakeware

baking dishes
Use a ceramic baking dish for recipes that require a more gentle heat, such as lasagnes, gratins and vegetable bakes. A metal baking dish, or roasting pan, is a much better conductor of heat so is best for cooking meat.

pie dishes
Choose from metal or ceramic. Metal gives a crisp, dry crust, while ceramic gives a softer one. Opt for deep dishes that will hold a generous filling. A lip on the dish makes securing a pastry top much easier.

ramekins
These ceramic cups are not only useful for cooking soufflés in, they can also be used for individual pot-pies and bakes, plus other pudding-style desserts. It helps to place ramekins on a baking tray before transferring them to the oven shelf, so they're easier to handle when hot.

tart tins
I like metal tart tins with fluted edges and removable bases. The fluting doubles the surface area of the pastry exposed to the heat, for faster baking.

cake tins
Aluminium (aluminum) tins are fine to use for baking, but stainless steel will last longer and won't warp or buckle. Always measure tin widths at the base, particularly when it comes to baking.

bundt
A decorative tin with fluted sides and a hole in the middle. A Bundt tin is used for dense cakes with a heavy batter. The hole in the middle allows the heat to penetrate the cake from all sides, baking it faster.

muffin
The standard sizes are a 12-hole pan, each tin with ½-cup (125ml) capacity, or a 6-hole pan, each tin with ¾-cup (180ml) capacity. The larger size are often known as Texas tins. Mini-muffin tins have a capacity of 1½ tablespoons. Non-stick tins make for easy removal, or line with paper cases.

round
The standard sizes for round cake tins are 18cm, 20cm, 22cm and 24cm. The 20cm and 24cm tins are the must-haves of this collection.

springform
With a loose base that is clipped and locked in, these round tins make removing cakes (especially cheesecakes) easy.

square
The standard sizes for square tins are 18cm, 20cm, 22cm and 24cm. If you have a recipe for a cake cooked in a round tin and you want to use a square tin, the general rule is to subtract 2cm from the size of the tin. For example, you would need a 20cm square tin for a recipe calling for a 22cm round cake tin.

frying pans and woks

deep frying pans
Fantastic for stir-frying vegetables and making pasta sauces. The larger capacity means you can add cooked noodles or pasta and toss them in the pan.

shallow frying pans
Good for cooking eggs and pancakes, simmering a sauce, searing a steak or dry-frying spices. Choose a frying pan with a thick base for even cooking and an insulated handle that won't heat up during cooking. A non-stick surface will minimise the amount of oil you will need when cooking. An ovenproof pan is useful for finishing cheese and egg dishes.

woks
Not essential, depending on your cooking style. A wok works best on a gas flame, which heats the base and sides – essential for good stir-frying. If you only have electric hotplates, it may be easier to stir-fry in a deep frying pan. A wok is also good for deep-frying. Choose stainless steel with a wooden handle if possible and season the wok before using it. By seasoning an uncoated metal wok at high heat with salt and oil, you'll help prevent food from sticking to it and the wok from becoming rusty.

knives, peelers and slicers

knives
The three most important knives a cook can have are a small paring knife, a cook's or utility knife and a serrated edge or bread knife. All do a variety of kitchen tasks. Choose a knife that feels well weighted in your hand.

peelers
A sharp vegetable peeler cuts the work of peeling a mountain of vegetables in half. Choose a good-quality peeler with a sharp blade. A wide one is good for peeling large vegetables such as pumpkin and for making vegetable ribbons. Also handy is a julienne peeler that shreds vegetables into very fine ribbons – they're super useful for making Asian salads and slaws.

slicers
Mandolines and spiralisers make slicing and creating vegetable 'noodles' really easy. They're not essential, but are handy to have and will save you prep time.

zesters
My favourite tool. When removing the zest from lemons, limes and oranges, use just a little pressure so that you are only removing the outer flavour-filled zest from the fruit, not the bitter white pith.

measuring equipment

measuring cups
Get a set that has 1 cup, ½ cup, ⅓ cup and ¼ cup measures. To measure dry ingredients with accuracy, fill generously and level off with the back of a knife. Cup measures differ between countries, so check the origin of the recipe you are using. For recipes in this book, consult the conversion chart on page 388.

measuring jugs
Essential for measuring liquids. Get one that has ml (fl oz) as well as cup measures. Measure the liquid at eye level on a flat surface for accuracy.

measuring spoons
Get a simple set that has 1 tablespoon, 1 teaspoon, ½ teaspoon and ¼ teaspoon measures. Level off the spoon after filling with dry ingredients for accuracy. Spoon measures differ between countries as they do for cup measures – see above.

scales
Indispensable for fast and accurate weighing of ingredients. Whether digital or conventional, a simple set will do.

other prep-ware

graters
I prefer a sturdy multifunctional box grater with various surfaces providing different grating options, rather than a different grater for each purpose. Choose stainless steel if possible and keep the fine surfaces clean with a small brush.

mixing bowls
Glass, metal or ceramic, a set of mixing bowls is essential. Glass and ceramic bowls may be preferable, as there is no limit to the time acidic ingredients such as lemon juice, vinegar and tomatoes can be kept in them (acidic contents may react with a metal bowl and acquire a metallic taste).

oven trays and pans

baking trays
Flat metal baking trays are great all-rounders – bake cookies, biscuits and galettes on them, use them under the grill (broiler), or utilise them in the preparation and assembly stages of cooking. Although most are non-stick, it helps to lightly grease and line trays with non-stick baking paper to be sure, plus it makes cleaning up so easy.

roasting pans
These vary in type and quality, from shallow and thin aluminium to thick, heavy-duty stainless steel. Choose a stainless steel pan, if possible, with deep sides; it will last a lifetime and has a good, even cooking surface.

power tools

blenders
A handy tool for pureeing soups, making smoothies, sauces and dressings. Heavy duty glass jugs are a must. A hand-held stick blender is perfect if you make lots of soups (and is also less messy than pouring soup into a blender!).

food processors
Use food processors to make pastry, blend foods, mix cakes, make breadcrumbs, cream butter and sugar or chop anything. They're the best all-round power tool if you only have space or budget for one. Small food processors are also handy for blending dips and sauces with ease.

racks

cooling racks
Usually made from steel or chrome-coated wire, racks are essential for cooling cakes, biscuits and tarts, as they let air circulate and prevent the 'steaming' process that can occur if some baked goods are left to cool in their tins. Line racks with clean tea towels or baking paper to ensure no marks imprint on delicate cakes like sponges.

roasting racks
Not only for cooling cakes, tarts and pies, ovenproof racks can be used to elevate meat in a roasting pan. Placing the meat on a rack means the heat from the oven can flow more evenly around the entire surface. It also prevents the meat from sitting amongst the fatty pan juices during roasting, and allows for any stock or wine to infuse moisture and flavour.

saucepans
Choose stainless steel saucepans with a thick base for even heat distribution and tight-fitting lids for a good seal. Invest in a few saucepans of better quality rather than a set of lesser-quality ones. Have a small size for sauces, a medium size for curries and vegetables and a larger one for boiling pasta.

utensils

spatulas
For turning, flipping and delicately removing or serving large wedges of food, I find a long, wide spatula is best.

spoons
From wooden to metal to slotted, you need a variety of spoons for a variety of kitchen jobs. Keep your sweet and savoury wooden spoons separate so that the flavour of heavy spices doesn't taint a delicate custard or cake. Keep a large metal spoon for folding and serving.

spoonulas
This spatula-and-spoon in-one is great for baking cookies and cakes.

tongs
Essential. Use them to toss pasta, turn steaks or chicken, mix or serve a salad.

whisks
When you're making soufflé, a smooth sauce or combining eggs, a medium-sized whisk with sturdy wires is a must.

GLOBAL MEASURES

Measures vary from Europe to the US and even from Australia to New Zealand.

METRIC AND IMPERIAL

Measuring cups and spoons may vary slightly from one country to another, but the difference is generally not sufficient to affect a recipe. The recipes in this book use Australian measures. All cup and spoon measures are level. An Australian measuring cup holds 250ml (8 fl oz).

One Australian metric teaspoon holds 5ml, one Australian tablespoon holds 20ml (4 teaspoons). However, in North America, New Zealand and the UK, 15ml (3-teaspoon) tablespoons are used.

When measuring liquid ingredients, remember that 1 American pint contains 500ml (16 fl oz) but 1 Imperial pint contains 600ml (20 fl oz).

When measuring dry ingredients, add the ingredient loosely to the cup and level with a knife. Don't tap or shake to compact the ingredient unless the recipe requests 'firmly packed'.

LIQUIDS AND SOLIDS

Measuring cups and spoons and a set of scales are great assets in the kitchen.

LIQUIDS

cup	metric	imperial
⅛ cup	30ml	1 fl oz
¼ cup	60ml	2 fl oz
⅓ cup	80ml	2½ fl oz
½ cup	125ml	4 fl oz
⅔ cup	160ml	5 fl oz
¾ cup	180ml	6 fl oz
1 cup	250ml	8 fl oz
2 cups	500ml	16 fl oz
2¼ cups	560ml	20 fl oz
4 cups	1 litre	32 fl oz

SOLIDS

metric	imperial
20g	½ oz
60g	2 oz
125g	4 oz
180g	6 oz
250g	8 oz
500g	16 oz (1 lb)
1kg	32 oz (2 lb)

MORE EQUIVALENTS

Equivalents for metric and imperial measures, plus ingredient names.

MILLIMETRES TO INCHES

metric	imperial
3mm	⅛ inch
6mm	¼ inch
1cm	½ inch
2.5cm	1 inch
5cm	2 inches
18cm	7 inches
20cm	8 inches
23cm	9 inches
25cm	10 inches
30cm	12 inches

INGREDIENT EQUIVALENTS

almond meal	ground almonds
bicarbonate of soda	baking soda
capsicum	bell pepper
caster sugar	superfine sugar
celeriac	celery root
chickpeas	garbanzo beans
coriander	cilantro
cornflour	cornstarch
cos lettuce	romaine lettuce
eggplant	aubergine
gai lan	chinese broccoli
green onion	scallion
icing sugar	confectioner's sugar
plain flour	all-purpose flour
rocket	arugula
self-raising flour	self-rising flour
snow pea	mange tout
white sugar	granulated sugar
zucchini	courgette

OVEN TEMPERATURES

Setting the oven to the right temperature can be crucial when making baked goods.

CELSIUS TO FAHRENHEIT

celsius	fahrenheit
100°C	200°F
120°C	250°F
140°C	275°F
150°C	300°F
160°C	325°F
180°C	350°F
190°C	375°F
200°C	400°F
220°C	425°F

ELECTRIC TO GAS

celsius	gas
110°C	¼
130°C	½
140°C	1
150°C	2
170°C	3
180°C	4
190°C	5
200°C	6
220°C	7
230°C	8
240°C	9
250°C	10

BUTTER AND EGGS

Let 'fresh is best' be your mantra when it comes to selecting eggs and dairy goods.

BUTTER

We generally use unsalted butter as it allows for a little more control over a recipe's flavour. Either way, the impact is minimal. Salted butter has a longer shelf life and is preferred by some people. One American stick of butter is 125g (4 oz). One Australian block of butter is 250g (8 oz).

EGGS

Unless otherwise indicated, we use large (60g) chicken eggs. To preserve freshness, store eggs in the refrigerator in the carton they are sold in. Use only the freshest eggs in recipes such as mayonnaise or dressings that use raw or barely cooked eggs. Be extra cautious if there is a salmonella problem in your community, particularly in food that is to be served to children, the elderly or pregnant women.

USEFUL WEIGHTS

Here are some simple weight conversions for cups of common ingredients.

COMMON INGREDIENTS

almond meal (ground almonds)
1 cup | 120g

brown sugar
1 cup | 175g

white (granulated) sugar
1 cup | 220g

caster (superfine) sugar
1 cup | 220g

icing (confectioner's) sugar
1 cup | 160g

plain (all-purpose)
or self-raising (self-rising) flour
1 cup | 150g

fresh breadcrumbs
1 cup | 70g

finely grated parmesan
1 cup | 80g

uncooked white rice
1 cup | 200g

cooked white rice
1 cup | 165g

uncooked couscous
1 cup | 200g

cooked shredded chicken, pork or beef
1 cup | 160g

olives
1 cup | 150g

index

thank you

THANK YOU

Creating a book like this is such a big production – I'm constantly reminded of the value of my incredible team. Some I've been working with for years and others are new to my projects, but all of them I consider to be masters in their craft. I'm so lucky!

To my photographer Will Meppem, your ability to capture light, colour and the beauty of fresh ingredients never ceases to amaze me. Thank you for your skill, patience and friendship. Stylist-extraordinaire Justine Poole, everything you touch turns to magic! Thank you, Juzzy, for your creativity and hard work, both on set and off, and for bringing my vision for this book to life.

Creative director, designer and the calmest of influences, Chi Lam – what would I do without you! You've expertly guided this project through every stage, from the initial concept to final proofs. I'm beyond grateful for your amazing eye, attention to detail and wisdom.

Abby Pfahl, thank you for your way with words. You ensure that each phrase is written beautifully and each recipe is edited flawlessly, with my sentiment shining through on every page.

Hannah Meppem, some days in the kitchen I swear you can read my mind! I love that you share my commitment to making every recipe taste and look so perfect. Shoot days are a thousand times easier when you're on set – I'm truly grateful for your proficiency and support. Hayley Dodd, you're a gem – thank you for calmly, happily and meticulously fine-tuning each recipe and for all your expertise throughout the shoots. You, Dolores Braga Menéndez, Maxwell Adey and Breesa Swann tested everything (and I know it's a big book!) to pure perfection. Huge thanks to all four of you.

In the prepress department, Tony Houssarini, your ability and commitment never go unnoticed. I'm ever thankful for the hours you spend helping to make these pages immaculate. My fabulous magazine team is very patient with me while I'm working on special ventures like this. Thank you all for being so encouraging, capable and hilarious – you're the best.

None of this would be possible without my team at HarperCollins*Publishers*. Shona Martyn and Catherine Milne, your faith in me is unwavering and I'm really appreciative of that. A big thank you must also go to Le Creuset, Smeg and KitchenAid for lending me their beautiful wares to feature in these pages.

Lastly, crafting *basics to brilliance* both for print and TV has meant this year was an extra busy one for me. My family and friends have kept me sane with their love and laughter. Your unquestionable support means the world to me – thank you. My two boys know how much I love them but thank you, Angus and Tom, for inspiring me and grounding me. You make each day so interesting, rich and (most importantly) fun as we juggle through our lives together.

BIO

Donna Hay is Australia's favourite and most trusted home cook and an international food-publishing phenomenon. Donna's 25 books have sold more than 6 million copies worldwide and have been translated into 10 different languages. In Australia, her recent books *Fresh and Light* (2012), *the new classics* (2013), *the new easy* (2014) and *life in balance* (2015) have dominated the bestseller charts. Her television cooking shows, including a new eight-part series based on the *basics to brilliance* book, have brought her signature style to life for viewers in more than 17 countries.

Donna Hay is a household name. She is editor-in-chief of *donna hay magazine* and creator of the number one magazine iPad app in Australia. Her column in the Sunday papers is read by 4 million readers in Australia every week. In addition, she is the creator of the donna hay for Royal Doulton collection, including homewares, plus her food range is stocked in supermarkets nationally. She is the working mum of two beautiful boys.

Books by Donna Hay include: *life in balance*; *the new easy*; *the new classics*; *Fresh and Light*; *simple dinners*; *a cook's guide*; *fast, fresh, simple.*; *Seasons*; *no time to cook*; *off the shelf*; *instant entertaining* and the *simple essentials* collection.

donnahay.com

For more of my cookbooks, plus plenty of super simple recipes for weeknights and weekends, visit donnahay.com. You can explore my online store of gifts, hampers, beautiful homewares and my collection for Royal Doulton, or create a gift registry for your next special occasion. Follow me on social media for news, inspiration and all the latest on the magazine and my blog.

Connect with Donna on Facebook, Twitter, Instagram and Pinterest

 facebook.com/donnahay   @donnahay   @donna.hay   pinterest.com/donnahayhome

WITHDRAWN